OUTRAGEOUS
CRICKET
MOMENTS

Ian Smith

OUTRAGEOUS CRICKET MOMENTS

The underhanded . . .
the undermined . . .
the underperforming . . .
and, of course, the UNDERARM!

with Joseph Romanos

Hodder Moa Beckett

National Library of New Zealand Cataloguing-in-Publication Data

Smith, Ian (Ian David Stockley), 1957 -
Outrageous cricket moments : the underhand, the undermined, the underperforming
and, of course, the underarm / Ian Smith with Joseph Romanos
ISBN 1-86958-934-3
1. Smith, Ian (Ian David Stockley), 1957- — Anecdotes. 2. Cricket—
New Zealand—Anecdotes. 3. Cricket players—Anecdotes.
I. Romanos, Joseph. II. Title.
796.3580993—dc 21

ISBN 1-86958-934-3

Published in 2003 by Hodder Moa Beckett Publishers Ltd
[a member of the Hodder Headline Group],
4 Whetu Place, Mairangi Bay, Auckland, New Zealand

Designed by Hodder Moa Beckett Publishers Ltd
Typesetting by BookNZ, Auckland
Printed by Printlink, Wellington

*This book is dedicated to
cricket lovers, young and old*

Contents

Introduction

When I set out to write this book, I didn't want it to be a sordid rehash of all the lowest and sourest moments in New Zealand cricket history. I like the term outrageous, but have used a fairly liberal definition of the word when considering stories for this book. I've included stories that I consider are outrageously funny, outrageously dramatic and outrageously bizarre, besides, obviously, the outrageously controversial.

This has enabled the story of the Ellis Park Massacre of 1953 to be examined, with new information courtesy of rare interviews with Bob Blair, Geoff Rabone and Bert Sutcliffe. There's also the still incredible account of the day New Zealand were dismissed for 26 in a test against England. Cricket historians will also be aware of the embarrassingly quick defeat by the star-studded Australian team at the Basin Reserve in 1946. There's a look at the dope-smoking scandal from the 1994–95 tour of South Africa, and the three bombings that ruined New Zealand cricket tours, two in Sri Lanka, one in Pakistan.

Counterbalancing these stories are accounts of happier and funnier times — our innings defeat of England in two days at Lancaster Park in 1984, Nathan Astle's incredible hitting display at the same ground against the same opponents in 2002, Peter Petherick's improbable hat-trick on test debut against Pakistan.

I've taken the opportunity to write about some of the players I spent a lot of time with during my career — Glenn Turner, Geoff Howarth, Richard Hadlee, Jeremy Coney, John Bracewell, Andrew Jones, Martin Snedden, Martin Crowe, Mark Greatbatch, Lance Cairns, Ewen Chatfield . . . they all feature prominently in these pages. Occasionally I've been critical of an aspect of their play, or of their actions, but I have great respect for the ability of all these cricketers and I hope that comes through strongly in the pages that follow.

Because a game of cricket takes all day, or all week, to complete, a lot of time is spent in the dressing room. There is ample opportunity for chat, for practical jokes, for black humour. Cricket is full of funny stories and I've done my best to include some of these. Jeremy Coney's antics when he was 12th man for New Zealand against Hampshire, Andrew Jones' reaction after scoring a test century in Australia, the ultra-competitive John Bracewell's sledging of his own players. These are memories I'll have with me throughout my life.

There have been some intriguing stories in our cricket history: Why did Rodney Redmond play just one test, in which he scored a century and a half-century? What was the story behind that over of Robert Vance's at Christchurch, the one that conceded 77 runs? How did a New Zealand team come to deliberately ball-tamper during a test match in Pakistan?

There's a pot-pourri of stories in this collection. The dismissal of Don Bradman by Jack Cowie, the controversy over 'chuckers', an examination of the players' strike in 2002, what it was really like to face Malcolm Marshall. A bit of this and a bit of that, rather like a game of cricket. Some straight deliveries, some spinners, a few swervers, the odd bouncer.

I've been in a fortunate position that has helped me write many of these stories. I spent more than a decade inside the New Zealand team dressing room and since then have made my living as a cricket commentator, in countries as widespread as England, India, Australia and various islands of the West Indies. During the course of my travels, I've been able to speak to many former players, and these discussions have provided a rich fund of stories of times gone by.

When I was a youngster playing junior rep cricket in Wellington, one of my team-mates was a portly opening batsman named Joseph Romanos. We once had a partnership of 90-odd against Hutt Valley at the Hutt Recreation Ground. Bruce Edgar, our star batsman, had been dismissed cheaply for a change, and that threw panic into the ranks. Fortunately Joseph and I had a good day, and our team won the match, and therefore the North Island under-14 title that season.

Since then Joseph and I have gone our separate ways, he into sports journalism and me primarily into cricket, as a player and a commentator. Our paths have crossed occasionally. One of the most enjoyable aspects of this book has been in having another partnership with Joseph, who has taken my stories, added some of his own, and helped produce this book, which I hope provides reading that is both lively and stimulating.

I'd like to thank a few other people who have helped in various ways. My wife Louise did much of my typing for me. And Keith Quinn, Tom Larkin and Don Neely provided either fresh stories or the flesh for the bare bones of stories I'd heard but wasn't sure about. Thanks also to News Media Auckland and Photosport who contributed so many photos to this book.

1. Of pay rates and strike rates

The players' dispute which shocked a sporting nation

The row between New Zealand Cricket and the Cricket Players' Association, which dominated radio talkback, television news bulletins and the front and back pages of newspapers for several weeks near the end of 2002, was one of the saddest chapters in New Zealand cricket history. A lot of outrageous statements were made during a protracted dispute that pitted friends against each other and could have ended the international careers of many of New Zealand's senior players.

I suppose a players' strike was inevitable at some stage. With cricket now a job for some New Zealand players, it's only natural that they would want as much pay as possible. It's like that in most areas of the workforce, so why would cricket be different?

Having said that, I must say my sentiments were entirely with New Zealand Cricket throughout the dispute. From my reading of the situation, Martin Snedden and other New Zealand Cricket officials bent over backwards to give players as much money as they could reasonably afford, while still being mindful of having enough funds to look after areas like women's cricket, junior cricket, coaching and umpires.

This was apparently not a consideration for the players — especially the international players — who wanted big pay rises come what may.

New Zealand's test players had got a whiff of what the leading Aussies earn and decided they wanted a piece of that sort of action. Never mind that the game in Australia brings in a vast amount more income from television, sponsors and advertisers, and never mind that the Australian players generally are much better performed than New Zealand's. The Cricket Players' Association, led by Rob Nichol,

Parore: Give players pay rise

■ CRICKET

FORMER Black Caps wicketkeeper Adam Parore says poor domestic pay

"You really do have to compromise your employment, to a significant degree. For $15,000, come on, that's pathetic," Parore said.

Key figures from both sides have been unwilling to comment and a dispute

with their coaches or associations till the dispute is settled.

play," he said. "That was a factor in my retirement despite the vastly increased revenue on the international scene."

revenue. It doesn't pull in big crowds or money for the TV.

"The international stuff has to fund it. So it's difficult for them [NZC] to

Selectors may have to pick second-string side

sumed they remain apart on the issue players — both don

light years the next tier of players tantalising amounts of money. when be an opportunity

Names that spring to mind in a backup Black Caps team are Richard Jones, Matthew Bell, Michael

NZC sees red over stumped pay talks

■ CRICKET
JONATHAN MILLMOW

NEW ZEALAND Cricket is considering suspending negotiations with the Players Association after another fruitless attempt at resolving the pay dispute yesterday.

The presence of a mediator in Wel-

▶ PAY STRI

Sept 27: The Dom reveals pay dispute Zealand Cricket an Association.

Oct 2: Players wi for the month an

Credibility on line for union man

Players'

Players body positive before pay talks resume

has taken anoth Zealand Cricket announcing the ly to return to

after accusing of breaking the the previously was endorsing and dandy. up for three ity in the public separate ages, coupled talking up lution. viewed with aland Crick- wedden, pre- m Friday's

difference o negotiat-

gards set- ulate and hich the alculated

his it is and en- it," Nichol

Snedden's focus remains the responsibility to all stakeholders in cricket from the Black Caps down to grassroots. Already 87 per cent of its take is spent on high performance.

"I don't accept what they see as a key

issue so that is quite a fundamental difference," Snedden said.

"Still I'm happy for them to put their case out there but I really won't know what it all means until we've sat down for a day or so — it is certainly not straight forward."

Talks resume in Wellington today and provision has been made for them to continue till tomorrow.

Nichol said their aim was to provide a counter offer to NZC's settlement proposal made on October 9.

The Players Association's initial demand was 40 per cent, or $2.6 million, and Snedden responded with a restructured payment deal costing NZC an extra $140,000.

Under NZC's offer leading first-class players could earn as much as $32,500 this season, while international players would be contracted on a five-tier payment system.

"We are very keen on putting a counter offer together, we're determined to get there," Nichol said.

Nichol denied there was any pressure from the players to go public with some information yesterday. The strike has been a public relations disaster for them and NZC has been free to deliver its side of the argument without being challenged.

"We are really happy with the way we have handled things and so are the players," Nichol said.

"We have never seen th in the public domain but o been half informed we would be better off fully in

Nichol also expressed negotiations had become

THE HEART OF NEW ZEALAND

THE DOMINION POST

Thursday, November 7, 2002

Petulant cricketers let the side down

JUST which part of "no" doesn't Rob Nichol understand? The spokesman for the Players Association, which

former United States president Ronald Reagan called the bluff of striking air-traffic controllers by sacking the lot and

▶ THE MAIN PLAYERS

New Zealand Cricket's bargaining team:
Martin Snedden (chief executive, pictured), John Graham (former manager) and Rob Davidson (Christchurch lawyer).

Provincial associations' bargaining team:
Ervin McSweeney (Wellington chief executive), Richard Reid (Canterbury chief executive).

Note: Players pay $100 management fee per annum to association.

New Zealand Cricket Players Association bargaining team:
Heath Mills (Auckland lawyer), Rob Nichol (Auckland lawyer, also runs rugby players' association), Andrew Scott-Howman (Wellington lawyer). **Note:** Nichol the main negotiator.

Players Association Board:
Dion Nash, Simon Doull, Roger Twose (pictured), Geoff Allott, Karl O'Dowda, David White (Auckland Rugby chief executive, independent), Nichol. **Note:** There is also a players advisory group comprising three senior Black Caps, one of which is believed to be captain Stephen Fleming.

WELLINGTON
Sharpening Services

Full sharpening services for:
○ Handsaws ○ Tungsten Blades ○ Retipping
○ ○ Garden Tools ○ Mowers, etc.

Strike could benefit Wilson

CRICKET
Duncan Johnstone

NEW ZEALAND cricket boss Martin Snedden won't be hauling anyone out of retirement to field a makeshift Black Caps side to face India but comeback allrounder Jeff Wilson could be an unexpected benefactor if the troubled pay negotiations break down. NZC has given the striking players a deadline of Tuesday to accept its improved offer. If they decline NZC will start targeting individual players and is prepared to go to any level to field a national team.

MARTIN SNEDDEN

Deal soon but at huge cost

Jonathan Millmow

OPINION

NEW ZEALAND Cricket and

who also spearheads the equivalent New Zealand rugby players' union, and Heath Mills (brother of cricketer Kyle Mills) seemed unwilling to accept those two key facts.

The same thing has happened in English county cricket, where there are hundreds of professional players, all living very comfortably, and most of them underperforming. Have a look at the England team's results over the past 15 years. For a country that boasts such a huge number of professional players, its results have been very mediocre.

I have no problem with great players being well paid. A Chris Cairns, fully fit and firing, deserves $300,000 a year. He is a match-winner and a crowd-pleaser, and brings in money through spectators and sponsors. But very few cricketers in New Zealand are even near that standard.

In essence, New Zealand Cricket offered about 50 players who are not good enough to play international cricket the chance to earn $25,000 or even more for maybe five months' work. That's an annual pay rate of $60,000, which is outstanding remuneration considering the players' standard.

The nature of professional sport is that if you play well, you get paid well. If cricketers do well playing for their provinces, they will break into the New Zealand team, and then be able to earn bigger money. That's as it should be. It's a rare apprentice who gets paid at a rate of $60,000 a year, which was the reality of the New Zealand Cricket offer that the players spurned for so long.

Watching from the sidelines, I thought the terms offered by New Zealand Cricket were very good. Domestic players were offered a very enticing rate of pay, they would have conceded in private. I'm sure the domestic players had to pinch themselves when they saw the sort of money they were being offered. Imagine how they felt when provincial teams started to be filled with lower-level players. I'll bet there were some urgent messages delivered to the New Zealand reps, something along the lines of: 'Hey, this is a great deal for us. You keep fighting if you want, but we want to get off the bus right now.'

The deal that was finally accepted was virtually the same as the one the players had walked away from so bitterly a week earlier. The one difference was that it was agreed 11 and not 10 players from each association would be contracted as professionals (excluding players with New Zealand Cricket contracts).

Yet when the players initially turned down virtually the same offer, Nichol said the dispute had gone beyond money, and was a point of principle. He talked about having to safeguard the future of cricket, expressed concerns about such matters as players switching associations and said there was a concern over junior cricket. Dion Nash weighed in with more invective.

Rob Nichol had seemed to get ever more intractable. Nothing worked. Negotiations stalled, a mediator got nowhere and deadlines came and went. It became frustrating to watch a person with no first class cricket background,

Nichol, jeopardising cricket's future, while Martin Snedden was unable to deal directly with the players.

Nash was, I assume, wheeled in to speak as a disgruntled former player. But Dion, in the interviews he gave, and at a big press conference in Auckland, did the players' cause more harm than good. He made some ludicrously bitter comments about how difficult it had been to deal with New Zealand Cricket over the past 10 years. This seemed irrelevant. New Zealand Cricket is a different beast these days. The Canterbury domination of previous decades has gone. Snedden and John F Reid, the bigwigs in New Zealand Cricket, are from Auckland. The days of autocratic dealings with the players belong in the past.

Nash claimed New Zealand Cricket had not treated its players well, and cited his own experiences when he was injured. 'Under Chris Doig [Martin Snedden's predecessor as New Zealand Cricket Chief Executive], New Zealand Cricket had an insurance scheme which paid a percentage of your costs when you were injured, but after that you were on your own. If you did not go with that insurance company you didn't get anything.' Premiums, he said, became very high if there was more than one injury. 'New Zealand Cricket is refusing to acknowledge there is a problem between itself and the players.'

Nash said he had problems with New Zealand Cricket from his first selection for the test side, during the 1992–93 season. He claimed that every year after that there were further problems.

'New Zealand Cricket had a very successful way of dealing with [problems like] that. They picked the top three or four players and paid them very well, and said, "The rest of you can go to hell."'

I was stunned by Nash's comments. Over the past decade I have travelled around the world, commentating on the New Zealand team's matches. In their moments of triumph, such as when they won the ICC Champions Trophy in Kenya, when they had the better of Australia in the one-day series in 2002 and when they beat England in a series in England in 1999, there wasn't the faintest suggestion that this was an unhappy, divided unit. They seemed to operate well together, to get on well and to respect each other. They never looked like victims of a New Zealand Cricket divide-and-rule policy.

Dion was always a very emotional, aggressive cricketer and he conducted himself the same way during the dispute. But what works on a cricket field isn't necessarily the best plan over a negotiating table. Some of his claims were torn apart by Chris Doig, when he decided to enter the fray. Doig suggested Dion was still carrying a chip on his shoulder after his failure to start a cricket players' association two years previously.

He recounted how he had at that time met 18 Black Caps in an Auckland hotel at Nash's request, and explained to the group that if they wanted to share the player-

Players on back foot

Parties remain upbeat on talks

Together again: Black Cap Chris Cairns and New Zealand Cricket chief executive Martin Snedden announce the agreement. Picture: THE PRESS

Fleming a winner on sticky wicket

CRICKET'S crippling pay dispute would have been settled long ago if players had become involved in talks in the coming weeks.

Attempts to better line the pockets of leading players appear to have failed, though both negotiating parties were upbeat at the completion of talks.

The NZCPA will provide NZC with a counter offer on Monday which will ultimately determine whether the players return to work next month.

The two parties are still poles apart on the contentious remuneration issue but logic suggests it will be the players that have to concede the biggest slice of ground if a resolution is forthcoming.

Much of yesterday's meeting at law firm Bell Gully focused on clarifying minor issues in regard to the player payment pool, but sufficient progress was made for further talks planned for today to be abandoned.

Negotiations will resume in Wellington next Wednesday.

Players Association spokesman Rob Nichol admitted there were

The dispute was quickly resolved after Black Caps captain Stephen Fleming and all the players

He also backed up his earlier claim that a resolution was still possible by the middle of next week. It seems a far fetched view unless they are prepared to concede defeat given the association had been calling for an increase of 60 per cent, or $2.8 million, and NZC responded with $140,000, or 3 per cent.

"Every time we meet we get closer,

week it will be fair and reasonable, otherwise we wouldn't be doing our job properly."

Nichol brushed off as speculation the view that the association wants the player payment pool to match Australia's and therefore be calculated on 25 per cent of NZC's turnover.

Apart from expenditure there is little comparison between the two countries and Australia's considerably bigger market giving them more

members for signing with associations.

The CPA rejected Snedden's initial

ously want the percentage based on net income but the Players Association may argue that that is open to manipulation.

"We don't expect to be paid as much as the Australians but we do want what is fair, and quite clearly at the moment we don't think the players are being recognised properly," Nichol said.

New Zealand Cricket chief executive Martin Snedden felt "some" common ground was reached.

"The bottom line is we won't know

acknowledged the CPA, and that we can get out and play some cricket," he

how much progress we've made until we receive their offer but I certainly felt decent progress was made.

"We've been exploring each other's position for quite a while now and clearly we don't accept each other's philosophy but we need a resolution to the issue."

Snedden's priority is to protect the stakeholders of the game, particularly grassroots which is at most risk from the players association's demands.

See BELL D4

Time to talk: New Zealand Cricket's negotiating team, from left, Ervin McSweeney, Rob Davidson, Richard Reid, Martin Snedden and John Graham arrive for talks with the Players Association yesterday. Picture: CRAIG SIMCOX

Snedden delivers payment proposal

■ CRICKET
JONATHAN MILLMOW

▶ NZ CRICKET'S OFFER
INTERNATIONAL
Contract 20 players:

NEW ZEALAND'S leading domestic

Cricketers' strike a sad indictment

Mystery on Sport with John Morrison

Greed and selfishness are not human traits we tend to associate with sport — team sports

Fleming: I couldn't sell my fellow players out

Stephen Fleming: Torn between peers and NZC.

Threats to his captaincy were raised but he could not comment on the future of Players Association spokesman Rob Nichol because he was "only one of 128 members".

However, he said he had Nichol's backing to make the approach to NZC which ultimately settled the stalemate.

Fleming decided to use former NZC chief executive Chris Doig as the go-between because he was "too nervous" about approaching Snedden direct.

The pair hadn't spoken since the player strike started on October 1, but Fleming said it was an amicable meeting.

Fleming, who has led his country in 47 tests and 122 one-day internationals, said during the low times he began looking at opportunities overseas.

"It started off being a humorous idea, but as things progressed the situation took on a more serious turn.

"There was no guarantee there was going to be a resolution and I was talking to contacts overseas. It was very difficult ... a very sad thought that I might not represent my country again."

More CRICKET D6

Players strike takes nasty turn

Threats to his captaincy were raised but he felt it was as hurtful as all the speculation was, he could never break ranks from the Players Association.

"I spent a lot time alone trying to work things out but essentially nothing could happen until both negotiating teams disengaged," he said. "It wouldn't have been worth captaining a side if I didn't have the trust of the players by selling them out. I couldn't do the job properly so I was damned if I do and damned if I don't."

Fleming set about restoring the game's credibility yesterday and clarifying his position in the Players Association. By mid-afternoon he had conducted 13 interviews but he acknowledged the best way to win back lost loyalty was through the top team's deeds on the park against India.

Bridges also need mending with some former players and there is his own relationship with NZC.

"There may be bridges to be built between us, but knowing Martin [Snedden — NZC chief executive] we will look to move forward."

payment pool among 100 players instead of 18, he would start to make the arrangements. The players apparently baulked at the idea.

Doig also said that, contrary to Nash's claims that he was not well-supported during his career, he was actually one of the principal beneficiaries of New Zealand Cricket's income insurance scheme and was well paid considering his haphazard availability. 'Dion's a hell of a good guy, but he's also emotive and he's not a very good loser,' said Doig. 'His claims are absolute rubbish and if they are an example of what's being fed to the players, well no wonder everyone is having problems.'

Doig said he was familiar with the remuneration packages for elite players and was flabbergasted when they turned down New Zealand Cricket's offer. 'The players need to know that what they're being offered is extraordinarily good and that they won't get any more money, whether they decide to play again or not,' he said. He was proved right.

'From what I've seen and heard so far, the Players' Association has completely lost the plot and is providing some very poor representation, which is a shame because the cricketers themselves are being damaged.'

Doig said that in his last year in office, 11 players were each paid more than $200,000. That is outstanding pay and made the players' determination to screw more money out of New Zealand Cricket all the more disappointing.

The Cricket Players' Association fought right to the end. They made noises about possible boycotts of New Zealand by other teams. But the International Players' Association scoffed at such suggestions. Then there was talk that India would not come to New Zealand if they could not be guaranteed top opposition. The Indians responded by saying they'd be touring come what may. It all served to undermine the Players' Association stance.

The players appeared greedy and unrealistic. My feeling was that the international players, having had a measure of success lately, felt they were in a position to push for more money.

What was even more disappointing was that they clearly had little feel for the game in New Zealand. In the way they negotiated it appeared they didn't care if the domestic programme was ruined, if the tour by India was thrown into jeopardy or even if preparations for the 2003 World Cup were thrown out of kilter.

It was interesting that our leading women's cricketers never entered the discussion. Rob Nichol and company were not interested in representing them, and the women made no equivalent pay demands. Indeed, they said they were very happy with how they were being looked after. Yet men's interprovincial first-class cricket in New Zealand does not draw any more spectators than do matches between our leading women.

Perhaps the women were just more realistic. As an aside, they are also the current world champions.

The other aspect of the pay dispute that staggered me was the Players' Association demand that New Zealand Cricket fork out $300,000 a year to fund the union. Since when should employers have to fund the union?

Personally I believe the whole situation would never have got out of hand if the players had represented themselves through a panel of current and past senior players of international and first-class standard. There was no need for Rob Nichol and co. It undermined Martin Snedden's ability to handle the whole deal. And he is, after all, the bloke who has represented the players' best interests superbly to this point, including during dicey situations such as the bomb blast in Karachi. Snedden is pro-cricket and always has been.

Nichol claimed the players were 100 per cent behind him and his endeavours. I don't buy that. I would imagine there were a number of nervous up-and-coming or fringe players who desperately wanted to pad up and get on with the game. They'd have broken out into a cold sweat when they saw second-tier players being offered their spots in various provincial teams. They'd have felt even worse when the Cricket Max and national Second XI competitions were scrapped because of the strike.

For a while there was a distinct possibility that New Zealand would field a sub-standard team for the tests and one-dayers against India. It appeared New Zealand might be represented by the Baby Black Caps during the summer of 2002–3.

If there was such unanimity among players, why did some of them take on the role of enforcers? From nearly every province, ugly stories emerged of young players being bullied and badgered by Players' Association members.

The players' leading representative should be the captain of the national team. Stephen Fleming was disappointingly quiet for far too long. It was noticeable that when he and Chris Cairns did finally get involved, the wrangle was quickly settled.

So why did the players cave in eventually? Was it because they cared about cricket, and wanted to ensure New Zealand was represented with honour against India and in the World Cup to follow? I doubt it. The big-name players lost their game of bluff because the court of public opinion was so strongly against them, and because the domestic players suddenly realised a harsh truth: other cricketers were being chosen to take their places. As soon as Canterbury and Otago filled their teams, and other provinces made noises about doing the same, the pressure was thrown back on to the recalcitrant players: did they want a well-paid job or not? It turned out they did. They ended their protest action quick-smart.

It was interesting to gauge the public reaction through the drama. From the letters to the editor I read, the talkback I heard and the people I discussed it with, it seemed that only about one person in 10 supported the players' stand.

Nichol seemed to me to be an obstruction. He is an accountant and has his Rugby Players' Association background. I just couldn't see that the cricketers needed him.

The final deal . . .

This is the deal the Cricket Players' Association eventually accepted:

A pool of $5.1 million for the contract period from June 1, 2002 to May 31, 2003; $3 million to the international player payment pool (an increase of 11 per cent) and $2.1 million to the domestic pool (an increase of 20 per cent).

New Zealand Cricket would allocate more than $330,000 to each of the six major associations, which would contract a minimum of 11 players, none of whom would be New Zealand Cricket-contracted. The contract period would be from October 1 until March 31.

Players would be ranked 1–11. Retainers would be $22,000 for players ranked 1–3, $14,000 (4–6), $8000 (7–11). Match fees for all players would be $1000 per State Championship four-day match, $500 per State Shield one-day match, and $250 per Max game. A captain's allowance would be $150 per game. Players ranked 1–3 could earn up to $37,500 in a season.

New Zealand Cricket would contract 20 international players to be ranked 1–20. Annual retainers would be $120,000 for players 1–3, $100,000 (4–6), $80,000 (7–10), $60,000 (11–15) and $40,000 (16–20).

Black Caps would receive $6000 per test and $2500 per one-day international, with no win bonuses. A captain's allowance would also be negotiated. Non-contracted players would receive $1000 per week while on an overseas tour with the Black Caps.

New Zealand Cricket-contracted players would receive the following benefits:

Coaching and technical assistance from New Zealand Cricket's high performance staff and use of facilities.

Travel (business class on overseas trips) and accommodation while assembled with the Black Caps.

Substantial playing, casual and formal clothing allocations.

Comprehensive fitness assistance and medical treatment.

Use of air points generated on travel paid by New Zealand Cricket.

Significant meal and laundry allowance while assembled with the Black Caps.

Benefits for players' partners, including limited free travel and accommodation and match hospitality.

Ticket allocation for international matches.

Access, through the Black Caps, to revenue opportunities from tournament or series prize money and sponsorship prizes.

All prize money won would be retained and shared by the players and management team.

The contract system agreed upon would remain in force for four years, from June 1, 2002 to May 31, 2006.

Player payments would be backdated and include the period from October 1, when the players began strike action.

He seemed to come out as a big loser in the whole debacle. Why was he not there at the end, when a solution was reached? Why did Fleming and Cairns get the credit for the deal going through? It appeared that Nichol had been sidelined, no matter what positive spin he tried to put on it.

All sorts of people weighed in to have their say. Every day, there'd be people who have been team-mates and friends in the cricket environment chipping at each other. Martin Crowe went public one day and criticised Fleming, saying Fleming needed to take over the pay negotiations. Crowe said Nichol, Mills and Nash had made a meal of the Cricket Players' Association negotiations. 'They've got to send in Stephen Fleming and Chris Cairns to replace Rob Nichol and Heath Mills at the negotiation table,' Martin said. 'Mills and Nichol have to step aside. They've failed, they don't have the credibility.'

Crowe said it was hugely damaging that Fleming and Martin Snedden weren't talking. 'They have not spoken for four months . . . can you believe that? It's staggering, and I know Martin Snedden's frustrated because he hasn't been allowed to. Stephen needs to be a mediator. You can't be that close to the players that you cannot be able to lead them and show them the right way.

'In my opinion the presentation of the players' case has been flawed. I seriously question the credibility of Nichol and Mills. I seriously question the rationale of Dion Nash. He's clearly the driving force behind them, but he just seems a little bit out of touch. I seriously question their decision to withdraw their services while they're in negotiations with New Zealand Cricket.'

In the end, the row, which had been building since negotiations began in May 2002, was settled on 11 November 2002. The domestic players received handsome pay rises, though nowhere near the amount they were seeking. The pay for the international players improved too, but not as dramatically. There was an increase in some retainers, but not as much movement in the overall amount the top players earn.

Advertising and world television rights income will inevitably fall over the next five to eight years. That is a worldwide trend. Just look what's happened in British and European soccer. New Zealand's ocean of financial resources, which looks quite deep just now, may well be a lot shallower in the years to come. Snedden and his board have tried to ensure the tide doesn't go out and stay out. They deserve credit for that.

Mercifully, we won't have to go through this shambles again soon, because the agreement struck is to last until 2006.

2. Personality clash added spice to historic victory

New Zealand's first test win against Australia

When I was at college, one of my cricket listening highlights was New Zealand's win over Australia at Lancaster Park in 1974. It was New Zealand's first test win against Australia and was especially sweet because for so long they'd refused to meet us at test level.

The Australian team was packed with big names and to a cricket-mad teenager, it seemed amazing that New Zealand could beat them. Following the game from afar and desperately hoping for a New Zealand win, there were lots of local heroes — Brian Hastings, Ken Wadsworth and Jeremy Coney all did things at the right time with the bat, while Richard Hadlee, Richard Collinge and Dayle Hadlee cut through such famous Australian batsmen as Stackpole, Redpath, Ian and Greg Chappell and Walters.

But the New Zealand hero, and the person who set up the history-making win, was undoubtedly Glenn Turner. He made 101 and 110 not out, and in a low-scoring match (no team reached 260) these were magnificent performances.

During the match, Turner also had a famous contretemps with Australian skipper Ian Chappell. Over the years, as I've got to know both people, I can see that a disagreement was entirely on the cards, for two more different personalities it would be hard to find.

Glenn was a professional cricketer by then, having played for Worcester for six or seven years. He didn't rate the Australians very highly because they weren't professionals. He thought their approach to cricket was amateurish. For their part, the Aussies wouldn't have been impressed by Turner. The Australians were

Teasing those Aussies. Ian Chappell (left), Ashley Mallett and wicketkeeper Rod Marsh appeal enthusiastically. Outstanding New Zealand batsman Glenn Turner wonders what all the fuss is about.

combative and liked to be fired up to perform well. Turner tried to take all the emotion out of his cricket.

Also, the Aussies suspected that Turner was shy about facing genuinely fast bowling. But that wasn't a factor at Christchurch because the Australians fielded a distinctly military medium attack, led by Max Walker and Geoff Dymock.

The Turner-Chappell spat occurred on the fourth evening. By then the Australians knew they were up against it. New Zealand needed 228 to win and went to stumps 177–4. Just before stumps Brian Hastings hoisted to the boundary. Umpire Bob Monteith signalled a six.

Non-striker Turner mentioned to him that the ball had landed inside the boundary and was just a four. Just as Turner was having this discussion with Monteith, a flustered Ian Chappell arrived, intending to set the umpire straight. He was annoyed to find Turner talking to the umpire. Turner told him he had sorted out things, which only annoyed Chappell more.

Chappell threw some choice swear words at Turner. Over the years the story grew so that some people claimed Chappell made racist comments about Glenn's wife, Sukhi. I was pleased to see that in Lynn McConnell's recent book, *The First Fifty*, Turner took the opportunity to set the record straight, saying no such racist comments were made.

The incident was quite nasty, though. In a backhanded way, it was a tribute to New Zealand, and Turner, in particular. The Australians did not like coming off second-best against New Zealand and I'm sure Chappell's outburst was borne partly out of frustration at an imminent test defeat and partly because he is one of the hardest buggers to have worn the baggy green.

3. When Braces put the bite on Franko

Fielding lapse earns a serve . . . and much mirth

Sledging between opposition players is a hot topic. It's commonplace and often funny and harmless, but there's no denying that at times it gets a little too pointed and damaging.

Far less common is sledging of team-mates, and when it happens it's generally good-natured and often very humorous. The funniest example of one team-mate sledging another happened while I was wicket-keeping for Auckland in a Shell Trophy match on the No 2 ground at Eden Park.

John Bracewell, champion off-spinner, was the bowler. Trevor Franklin, all six foot six inches of him, was a very unwilling close-in short point. I should say right now that it's not an easy position to field. You need a desire to be there and a low point of gravity to ensure you can move quickly.

Franko, great bloke though he is, possessed neither attribute. (He did, however, have a magnificent appetite, especially for a top-order batsman.)

After a succession of close calls with bat/pad and pad/bat deflections, Braces was getting a little miffed, irritated even, by Franko's lack of action.

First he suggested loudly that if the ball had mayonnaise and sauce on it, Franko would show more interest in wrapping his hands around it.

That produced some smiles among the Auckland fieldsmen perched around the bat. But Braces really broke up the whole field 10 minutes later. After seeing a couple of other chances go begging in the vicinity of short point, John simply lost it. To be fair, Franko was a little late reacting, but by then it was obvious he was getting a tad peeved himself.

John Bracewell . . . you crossed him at your peril.

Braces took a pace down the wicket and demanded loudly of his captain, Jeff Crowe, who was doing his best to contain himself at first slip, 'Chopper, would it be possible to have another statue at short point?'

Jeff couldn't reply or act. Like the rest of us he was on the deck laughing.

All except Franko, of course, who instantly backtracked to a deeper point and was never to be found in the inner sanctum again.

4. Getting the bum's rush — Aussie style

Greg Chappell's unique answer to the streakers

We have a curious attitude to streakers. Officially, we frown on them. They're attention-seekers, usually drunk attention-seekers. They waste time, distract the players and all that. Television networks around the world generally choose not to show footage of streakers any more, feeling that if they get air time, it will only encourage others.

When a streaker runs on to the field now, the television cameras seem to cut away to a close-up of the batsman's helmet, while commentators earnestly discuss tactical nuances that are unfolding. All the while, viewers at home can hear cheering and shouting.

However, while it's good to be mature and sensible about these things, there's no denying that down the years streakers have enlivened many a dull afternoon at the cricket.

One of the most famous of all streaks happened at Lord's in 1975, during the second Australia-England test that season. Streakers were a novelty back then and the naked gentleman's appearance caused an uproar. Fortunately, the maestro, John Arlott, was at the microphone.

Without pause to think, Arlott said: 'And we have a freaker . . . not very shapely . . . and it's masculine . . .'

Richie Benaud was commentating during a Prudential Cup match at Edgbaston, England one time. Australian wicketkeeper Rod Marsh had had a nightmare day, having dropped two catches off Terry Alderman's bowling, when a streaker raced on to the ground. As Marsh tackled the streaker (with a copybook technique that any rugby player would have been proud of) Benaud was heard to remark, 'It's probably the only ball Marsh has cleanly gloved all day.'

Greg Chappell didn't like streakers at all. He'd shown his intolerance of them several times even before he led Australia on a two-test tour of New Zealand in 1977.

Chappell was clearly annoyed when a streaker disrupted proceedings during the first test at Christchurch, and tackled a naked man who was attempting to get over the fence, then whacked him on the backside. The streaker turned and grabbed Chappell's cap and Chappell set out after him again.

'I took his hand and didn't let go,' said Chappell. 'When he realised the police were coming he tried to get away, so I gave him a whack or two to quieten him down.'

When another streaker appeared during the second test, at Eden Park, he took action again. At the time Chappell and Rick McCosker were putting the test beyond New Zealand's reach. They'd added 115 runs when a student, wearing only headphones, ran towards the stumps.

Chappell, on 58, beckoned the streaker towards him. 'I didn't know if he was going to try and souvenir a bail or some stumps,' Chappell said later. 'I put my hand out to shake hands with him, which he accepted. I had my bat in my left hand and gave him a couple of sharp cracks across the buttocks just to try and get him to stand still. Finally the police got there and took him away.'

The incident disrupted the test for several minutes and clearly affected Chappell's concentration, for he was run out moments later when he was too slow to respond to a routine call from McCosker.

Chappell one time grabbed a trouser-less man by the hair, and hung on for several minutes, marching him to the fence to be arrested.

Eventually, players were cautioned to leave the nude invaders to the police. Legal advisers warned that streakers could sue for damages if they were injured. It would have been interesting to see how Chappell dealt with a female streaker.

England seems to breed streakers. One even appeared at St Andrew's during a Tiger Woods round at the British Open golf, and there was the well-documented incident just before the 1996 Wimbledon men's singles tennis final. A shapely 23-year-old London student, Melissa Johnson, climbed over a barrier and dashed past finalists Richard Krajicek and MaliVai Washington as they posed near the net for photographs. Johnson was topless and wore only a tiny maid's apron, which she

Greg Chappell tended to dispense summary justice to streakers.

lifted up. She was quickly escorted off the court near the Royal Box by two policemen. Both players broke into laugher, as did most of the 14,000 fans.

Perhaps the most famous of all streakers was Erica Roe, who braved a chilly January day at Twickenham in 1982 to streak at halftime during an Australia-England rugby test. Roe, amply endowed, is now married with three children and is an organic farmer living in Portugal. Her streak caused a sensation and in a recent poll was ranked No 71 among England's top 100 sports highlights of all time.

There has been a surfeit of streaking in cricket in England too. There were four separate streaking incidents on the Saturday of the England-West Indies test at Old Trafford in 2001.

A determined male streaker caused some amusement for the crowd, and the New Zealand fieldsmen, when he interrupted proceedings during the fourth test at the Oval in 1999, the one in which New Zealand outplayed England to wrap up the series.

During the 1999 World Cup, when New Zealand and South Africa met at Edgbaston, the game was interrupted for quite some time while a bout of streaking was dealt with.

Closer to home, there's been no shortage of streakers, either. Early in the 2000 women's cricket World Cup, a rather ordinary England-Sri Lanka clash at the Brierley Oval was brought to life for a few minutes by a male streaker.

And during the 2002 season, when Australia and New Zealand played that wonderful women's one-day match at the Bert Sutcliffe Oval (Australia, chasing 253, won on the last ball), a jockstrapped streaker enlivened proceedings.

During the New Zealand-Pakistan one-dayer at Carisbrook on 28 February 2001, a streaker ran on to the field, and held up play to shake the hand of New Zealand bowler Chris Harris at the top of his mark before being tackled and escorted off the field.

Of recent streaks, the Perth test in December 2001 was as memorable as any. The test was notable for the century on debut by Lou Vincent and the fact that four New Zealanders — Vincent, Stephen Fleming, Nathan Astle and Adam Parore — scored centuries in the first innings. New Zealand outplayed Australia and threatened to win the match.

Those who were there will also recall the efforts of several streakers, including some determined women, who supported New Zealand, and waved a New Zealand flag in patriotic fashion as they raced around the ground naked. The fines for streaking in Australia are considerable — in excess of $A5000. So before people streak there these days, they have to ensure they have good financial backing from their mates, otherwise the whole exercise becomes far too costly.

5. Zing went the swing on Pring's ball

New Zealand guilty of ball-tampering

This is a story about a time the New Zealand team deliberately bent the rules. It happened in 1990, during our tour of Pakistan. By the time we got to Faisalabad for the third test, we were really on a hiding to nothing.

The Pakistanis were simply too good for us, especially as our team lacked John Wright, John Bracewell, Jeff Crowe, Richard Hadlee, Andrew Jones and Martin Snedden, who'd all either retired just before, or made themselves unavailable.

The Pakistani pace bowlers, especially Wasim Akram and Waqar Younis, were getting amazing reverse swing. Our quickies, Danny Morrison, Willie Watson and Chris Pringle, were getting virtually no movement after the first few overs.

During the test at Lahore, we got lucky by receiving a big clue as to how Pakistan's bowlers might have been getting some help. Towards the end of the test, Pakistan took the new ball. The umpires gave the Pakistanis the new ball and, as is usually the case, rolled the old one off the park. The local officials were a little slow to pick up on the fact that the old ball was sitting on the boundary edge and for once we beat them to the punch, grabbed the ball and smuggled it into our dressing room for inspection.

There was little doubt it was uniquely damaged on only one side. It had been scratched by something — long scratches too. We took a couple of quick photos before the local officials tried to thwart our plan by retrieving the ball. But we'd had time to formulate some methods of our own.

So prior to the next test, in Faisalabad, Martin Crowe and a few of the bowlers began experimenting in the nets, scratching one side with a bottle top. Chris Pringle, in particular, started getting a vast amount of swing. Even us mere part-timers were

Chris Pringle . . . champion New Zealand ball-tamperer.

able to swing it. Chris decided to have some fun in the next test, and he certainly did.

He put a piece of bottle top in his pocket and used it to scratch the ball, at drinks and at the fall of each wicket. The ball began to swing for him, and he found he was also getting much more movement off the wicket. None of our bowlers could get reverse swing — they weren't quite quick enough for that. But Pringle got so much assistance from the roughed-up ball that that didn't matter. He took 7–52 in the first innings, 4–100 in the second. I'll go as far as to say Pringle bowled as well in that first innings as he had ever bowled — it was Hadlee-like.

There is little doubt that this was one of the earliest and most open examples of ball-tampering, and following Pringle's unashamed admissions in interviews and his biography, the cricket world became, for better or worse, a lot more informed about this practice. Umpires were instructed to become more vigilant out in the middle.

These days, when wickets fall the umpires are handed the ball so that during the break it is no longer possible to have an unnoticed concerted crack at the ball.

Of course, there have been other examples of ball-tampering, with the infamous Mike Atherton dirt-in-the-pocket being the most-publicised. I guess we could have been more secretive about our exploits, but history will say that was not the Pringle way.

6. Suicide to 'salvation' for 10-wicket hero

The strange case of Mr Moss

The name of A E Moss has stared out from the pages of the *New Zealand Cricket Almanack* since it was first produced in 1948. Alfred Moss remains the only bowler in New Zealand first-class cricket history to have taken 10 wickets in an innings. He did so on 27 December 1889, playing for Canterbury against Wellington at Hagley Park, Christchurch. Thus his figures that day, 10–28, have remained the best ever returned by a New Zealand bowler.

Behind the bare entry of 'A E Moss' lies quite a story.

He emigrated to New Zealand to escape tuberculosis, which was ravaging his family in England. In New Zealand, his fast bowling soon earned him a place in the Canterbury team. His dream day occurred on his debut for Canterbury and the ball was later mounted and presented to him to recognise his wonderful feat.

Unfortunately, he suffered a fall from grace not long after his record bowling feat. He was a compulsive, though secret, drinker and his young schoolteacher wife left him when she found out, taking his prized cricket ball with her. Shamed and broken, Moss moved to South America, then on to South Africa.

Drinking cost him job after job until, on the point of suicide, he visited the Salvation Army in Cape Town. It turned his life around. For the next 50 years, he worked for the Salvation Army.

I wasn't there at the time, so can't vouch for this, but the story goes that his wife read of a Captain Moss of the Salvation Army in South Africa working with alcoholics. She traced him and they corresponded for some time. In 1915, while living at Rondebosch, a parcel arrived for Moss — it was the mounted cricket ball.

The 1890 Canterbury baseball team that included five provincial cricket reps. Albert Moss is seated in the centre of the front row and at the back left is Leonard Cuff, a New Zealand cricket captain and founder of the Olympic movement in Australasia.

What is sure is that she joined him in South Africa and when she became an officer in the Salvation Army, they remarried.

Albert Moss died at the age of 92 on 11 December 1945.

Merrins masters of the generation game

This feat has possibly been matched elsewhere, but surely not too often. Conway ('Cocky') Merrin and his son Russell both represented North Canterbury in the same match. Two decades later, Russell and his son, Gary, repeated the feat, also playing for North Canterbury in the same match.

I've known the odd family where father and son have played together at representative level — Lance and Chris Cairns are the most well-known example — but to have three generations involved is far rarer.

7. Underarm, underhanded ... and unforgiven

The delivery that horrified a nation

The most famous cricket match New Zealand has ever played, and the one which really kicked off cricket's rock era of the 1980s, happened at Melbourne on 1 February 1981. It has become known as the Underarm Match and it's amazing to me to think that it happened more than 20 years ago. If you aren't 30 years of age now, you probably have little or no memory of watching it live.

It's a funny thing — we lost the match, but we emerged as heroes. The controversy at the end of the match, when Australian captain Greg Chappell ordered his younger brother Trevor to bowl the last delivery underarm to Brian McKechnie, was so intense that it enveloped everyone — the media, the public, politicians, law-makers in England, even people who really were not remotely interested in cricket.

Cricket in New Zealand had never received such publicity and suddenly the game attracted hundreds of thousands more followers. Television ratings for cricket, one-day internationals especially, rocketed, there were some overflow crowds at home in the years that followed and the players themselves became public personalities.

In a way it came at the right time for New Zealand cricket. We'd been gradually improving through the 1970s and by the time we beat the West Indies at home in 1980, we had a solid international team. Players like John Wright, Geoffrey Howarth, Bruce Edgar, Jeremy Coney, Lance Cairns and Ewen Chatfield had developed into world-class cricketers. There was a new group, including John Bracewell and myself, with the Crowe brothers Jeff and Martin waiting in the wings, hungry for opportunities. And, of course, we had The Champion, Richard Hadlee, the player who gave us that match-winning edge. The basis was there for a New Zealand team

Moment of shame No 1: Martin Snedden about to make a brilliant outfield catch to dismiss Greg Chappell. Snedden's catch was inexplicably disallowed.

that could tackle any opposition with realistic hopes of victory.

So the time was ripe; it just needed something to light the flame. The Underarm Match did it.

It had been a long summer in Australia, with 10 one-dayers against India and Australia, a three-test series against Australia, sundry other outings against state teams and various selections, and finally, the one-day finals.

With the matches being shown back home live in prime time, interest was high. It increased further when we thrashed Australia in the first final. Hadlee knocked them over, taking 5–26 in eight overs and that was that. Brian McKechnie supported him with 3–23 off nine overs and Australia's batting crumbled. We won by 78 runs.

But as good as we felt after that first final, at Sydney, we felt equally bad two days later after they levelled the series by hammering us by seven wickets. We were bowled out for 126. Only Bruce Edgar reached 20.

The third one-dayer (remembering it was a best-of-five series) was played the next day, a Sunday, again at the Melbourne Cricket Ground (MCG). More than 52,000 paying people turned up that day and the atmosphere was intense.

They batted first and made 235–4, which was a very competitive score back then. However, their innings contained a sensational incident. Greg Chappell, playing well, was batting us out of the match. He and Graeme Wood eventually added 145 for the second wicket, but when Chappell reached 58 he was out, caught at mid-wicket by Martin Snedden.

It was a great catch. Martin ran in from the boundary about 30 metres and dived forward, skidding on his elbows after he took the ball centimetres above the ground.

We rushed over to celebrate with him because we knew Chappell was the key wicket. Then, amazingly, Chappell wouldn't depart. He stood his ground and umpires Cronin and Weser consulted, then gave Chappell not out. We were dumbfounded. Our skipper, Geoff Howarth, protested vigorously, and so did senior player Mark Burgess. But it didn't do us any good. They both said they'd been watching for short runs and hadn't followed the ball.

I really couldn't think of a similar example in big cricket. Generally — certainly until the last few years — the batsman if in doubt will ask the fieldsman if he's caught it, and will then accept his word. Snedden's every reaction indicated it was a fair catch, but Chappell wouldn't accept that. Despite the urgings of many of our players, Chappell stood unrepentant and seemingly unaffected by the whole affair.

Standing next to him in my keeping role, I was amazed at just how cool he was. He stood almost motionless, just leaning on his bat waiting for others to sort it out and at no stage did he contemplate consulting anybody.

Looking back it seemed an interesting state of mind he was in — later events would reveal just how interesting.

Television replays later showed it was clearly a good catch. Richie Benaud was commentating on Channel 9 at that moment. He's not prone to dishing out superlatives easily but he did describe the catch as 'one of the greatest outfield catches you are ever likely to see'.

AGC Finance later produced a series of still photographs in the form of a poster, which later displayed the incident perfectly. Signed by both Snedden and Chappell, they would be valuable collectors' items today. With all the fuss at the end of the game over the Underarm, that incident is often overlooked. It shouldn't be. It was the critical moment of the match. Chappell lost a lot of respect in our eyes for not going after he'd been caught.

So Chappell continued. Getting him out once when he was in that form was hard enough, twice was really asking a lot. He got through to 90 when, ironically, he was dismissed after another superb outfield catch, this time by Bruce Edgar. This time Chappell didn't query it. He'd done the damage.

So we were all pretty hot when the Aussie innings finished, and were very determined to have the last say.

Our innings began well when Wright and Edgar put on 85, but after that we lost wickets regularly. Bruce continued to bat stylishly at one end, scoring steadily. But no one really stayed with him. He brought up his century just before the end and when we began the last over we needed 15 to win and had four wickets in hand.

I think Greg Chappell must have counted his overs wrong somewhere, because it seemed a little strange that he would have Trevor Chappell bowling at the death when

Moment of shame No 2: Trevor Chappell (left) turns after bowling the infamous underarm delivery to Brian McKechnie, who has hurled his bat away in disgust. Neither wicketkeeper Rod Marsh nor non-striker Bruce Edgar seems especially happy at what's gone on.

his attack included Dennis Lillee and Max Walker. As it happened, Trevor Chappell bowled a pretty good over.

Hadlee belted one and was then out lbw and I strode out intending to win the match for us. I hit two consecutive twos, but was out straight after, clean bowled slogging wildly across the line. So that left one ball to be bowled and us needing seven to win, six to tie. Some people think that a six would have won us the match, but that's not so. We needed a six just to tie.

Brian McKechnie was the next batsman. His was a hopeless task. He was going to have to go out there and club a six first ball in one of the biggest cricket stadiums in the world. It had been such a gripping match all day that we were all very emotional. And with cricket, you never know. . .

McKechnie had once kicked a last-minute penalty from the sideline to win us a rugby test against Wales, so . . . what's the expression: cometh the hour, cometh the man.

That's when Greg Chappell pulled his underarm trick. When I think back to those dramatic moments, snapshots run through my mind. There was Aussie wicketkeeper Rod Marsh waving his arms and apparently imploring Greg to change his mind.

There was non-striker Edgar's obvious disgust when it became apparent what was going to happen. You had to feel for him. He was stranded at the non-striker's end with an unbeaten century to his name — almost overlooked to this day. He had been largely responsible for getting us that close in the first place.

Then Trevor bowled the ball, McKechnie blocked it — he said later the ultimate ignominy would have been to be bowled — and then he threw away his bat in frustration.

It was a two-tiered dressing room at the MCG in those days. Inside, there was chaos, upstairs and down. Mark Burgess biffed his cup of tea at the television. John Bracewell was, predictably, particularly vehement. At that moment Australia was not his favourite country and Greg and Trevor Chappell were emphatically not his favourite people. Most of the team were fairly disgusted.

I'd just got back to the dressing room and was still in my pads watching all this. Howarth ran past me in his socks, fly undone and raced on to the field to talk to the umpires. He thought what the Chappells had done might have been illegal.

In the commentary box, Ian Chappell made no bones about it. He was very critical of brother Greg's handling of the situation.

Amid the pandemonium immediately after the match, a group of Australian officials came into our dressing room. They were embarrassed and wanted to apologise. We had a big New Zealand flag laid out on the dressing room floor and they walked right over it, which only inflamed feelings further.

There was a macabre scene an hour or so later when we left the MCG. Though we'd lost the game, we were treated like heroes by the hundreds of people who had hung around to cheer us and let us know they didn't agree with what the Aussies had done. Here we were in Australia. We'd lost, but we were the heroes and they were the villains.

I must say that I wasn't as emphatic about it as some of our team. What Greg had ordered wasn't against the laws of cricket, though it brought about a change to the laws the next year. I think as a youngster I felt stunned by the events of the whole day.

I suppose it had been such an enthralling game and had see-sawed right down to the last over that people got very caught up in it and felt they'd been robbed of the game's natural climax by the Aussies playing fast and loose with the game's ethics.

We had no idea of the impact that game — that one delivery — would have. We went to Sydney for the next final and were greeted like conquerors, even though we lost.

Outside cricket, everyone seemed to have an opinion. New Zealand Prime Minister Rob Muldoon came out with his famous remark about it being appropriate that the Aussies were wearing yellow uniforms. Australian Prime Minister Malcolm Fraser was questioned and he said he was annoyed at the Aussie tactics too.

The Melbourne *Age* said: 'Australian cricket is in disgrace and the country's reputation as a sporting nation is severely damaged.' *The Australian* was equally critical: 'It . . . has since been described as shameful, spineless, disgraceful, churlish and gutless. The Australian sporting image has been tarnished as never before.'

Back in New Zealand, the underarm delivery seemed to be about the only topic of conversation for a few weeks. The fact that Australia was a nation descended from convicts was mentioned more than a few times.

When we arrived back in New Zealand for the series against India, it was noticeable how much more interest there was in the cricket. The crowds were bigger and cricket was the hot topic.

The following season the Australians toured. Greg Chappell captained them again and in the first match, a one-dayer at Eden Park, he was booed roundly as he walked out to bat. Chappell, a master batsman, answered in style, though, with a beautiful century, and returned to the pavilion to rousing applause.

That was the afternoon when a spectator threw a lawn bowl on to the playing area and Jeremy Coney, always quick to see the humour of a situation, retrieved it and under-armed it back.

Trevor Chappell, Brian McKechnie and, sometimes, Bruce Edgar, three of the principals of the Underarm, have started almost a cottage industry down the years. It appears that on 1 February each year since there has been some sort of Underarm Reunion. McKechnie must have racked up the air points and made a fortune telling his side of the story. Trevor has been to New Zealand a couple of times at least to film commercials and to speak. It's difficult even today to work out whether he was a victim or a villain. Do you refuse your captain? Isn't that mutiny?

When we did the video cricket history *From Cloth Cap to Helmet*, McKechnie hammed it up, showing viewers what he should have done. He put his box down on the pitch and when the ball hit it and flicked up, he swiped it out of the ground.

I think Greg Chappell suffered the most trauma over the years. Immediately after the game he said, 'It was a spur of the moment decision and I was mindful of what I was doing . . . It is within the rules of the game — it is fair play.'

Later, perhaps as the consequences set in, he changed his tune. He said he regretted his decision and that it was wrong. He explained his state of mind, saying it had been a long summer and that he was at the end of his tether and desperate for victory to try to finish the finals as quickly as possible.

It's all history now, and always worth a laugh when the subject is raised. Every time the Australians do something we don't like, such as winning the rights to host the 2003 rugby World Cup, you hear New Zealanders say they've 'done an underarm' on us. The expression has become part of the language and is often used with humour.

It was a lot different back in 1981 when New Zealand was a country outraged, and two Prime Ministers became involved.

8. Selectors deal our worst tour hand

Curly calls aplenty in our team of '37

The 1937 New Zealand team to England is not recalled particularly fondly by cricket historians. Curly Page's side failed to win a test and did not greatly distinguish itself in games against the counties, losing seven of these games and winning only four.

It's not the players who should have been criticised, though, but the selectors, for this was quite possibly the worst selected New Zealand touring side.

The selectors, Alf Duncan, Nessie Snedden, Harry Whitta and Johnny McMullan, managed to omit about eight of New Zealand's outstanding cricketers, and this at a time when New Zealand cricket did not have much depth.

Four key players, Stewie Dempster, Roger Blunt, Ken James and Bill Merritt, were overlooked because of an edict from the New Zealand Cricket Council prohibiting cricketers playing professionally in England from selection. This ruled out in Dempster and Blunt two of the all-time great New Zealand batsmen; James, one of the finest wicketkeepers in the world; and Merritt, a world-class leg-spinner who had already made two highly successful tours of England.

The selectors then compounded the problem by indulging in a series of parochial trade-offs and by failing to do their homework properly.

They omitted both Ted Christensen and Tom Pritchard, two of the country's best fast bowlers. Christensen had done great things for Taranaki and Pritchard was in devastating form for Manawatu, but the selectors never bothered with them. In fact, they had one opportunity to see Pritchard playing for Manawatu, but elected not to get off their train when it stopped in Palmerston North.

Also overlooked were Paul Whitelaw and Ken Uttley. Whitelaw, of Auckland, that

Don Neely Collection

Tom Pritchard . . . why didn't they want him?

season won the Redpath Cup, having scored 410 runs at an average of 82. Uttley, of Dunedin, was a consistently good batsman, very strong off the back foot. He won the Redpath Cup the following season and was one of the country's best batsmen right through until the Second World War.

Merv Wallace, who was the leading batsman in that 1937 team, was always emphatic that the selectors blundered badly that year.

He wrote in his book *A Cricket Master*: 'If you put in Dempster, Blunt, James, Merritt, Pritchard, Christensen, Whitelaw and Uttley and add them to the top players who did make our touring team, you would have had the basis of a great team. It is often said, quite rightly, that New Zealand cricket enjoyed a golden era in the 1980s, but it might have been a different story if the selectors had chosen a team that was missing John Wright, Martin Crowe, Ian Smith, John Bracewell, Bruce Edgar, Jeff Crowe, Ewen Chatfield and Lance Cairns. That's what it was like in 1937. No wonder we struggled.'

There were other problems in 1937. Ian Cromb was expected to captain the side, and had led New Zealand well the previous season. But Curly Page emerged from retirement and Cromb was omitted altogether. Wellington leg-spinner Bernie Griffiths was chosen then dropped at the last moment because it was decided — not by him — that he needed dental treatment. The Palmerston North Chamber of Commerce raised some money and Manawatu left-arm spinner Norm Gallichan was included in his place. Griffiths was understandably shattered.

When you hear stories like this, you realise how far we have progressed in terms of selecting teams. These days you can argue the merits of one player against another, but at least the best players are considered, all candidates are seen, money is not a factor in one player being chosen ahead of another and parochialism seems to have largely been removed. That's progress.

9. Newspaper story heralds shock withdrawal

Selector (and player) Snedden makes his stand

Imagine what today's talkback callers would make of this story, concerning Nessie Snedden, one of the early giants of New Zealand cricket and the grandfather of Martin Snedden, the current chief executive of New Zealand Cricket.

Nessie Snedden first played for New Zealand in 1913 and over the years proved himself a very good all-rounder, as well as a clever thinker on the game. He led Auckland very successfully for some years and in the early 1920s filled the dual role of New Zealand selector and captain.

In 1923 New Zealand played a three-match series against the legendary Archie MacLaren's MCC team. Snedden scored 5, 10, 0 and 58 in the first two internationals and picked up three wickets, but did not play in the third match for reasons that reveal much about his character.

The New Zealand selectors chose their side for the third 'test' and agreed to confirm it to each other by telegraph after the MCC-Wellington fixture, before it was announced to the press. Snedden, therefore, was surprised to read in the *New Zealand Herald* the next morning the announcement of the team without his okay.

Worse, veteran Wellington played Stan Brice, who took 10–97 against the MCC, had not been chosen.

He cabled fellow selector Ken Tucker: 'Surprised you published team without reference to me. Consider Brice should replace McBeath. I have resigned selectorship. Will not play third test.'

Ironically, Brice was duly selected for the match, replacing Snedden. If talkback

News Media Auckland

Nessie Snedden . . . resigned on principle.

radio was able to have a feast with Richard Hadlee's fictional answerphone message to Adam Parore in January 2002 — 'Don't come Monday' — imagine what it would have done with the Snedden situation?

Snedden continued playing for Auckland until 1928. Apparently the wounds caused by the selectorial contretemps healed quickly. He was back on the national selection panel in 1925 and continued selecting teams until 1937.

10. Flem's tactics prove point on bonus

Skipper Fleming left few options in VB Series

The Australians were drawing a long bow when they complained about Stephen Fleming's tactics during the 2002 VB Series. If you remember, New Zealand elected to lose to South Africa by a large margin in their final game of the one-day series, making it much harder for Australia to make the final.

It all seems a bit complicated, but stick with me and you'll understand . . .

When New Zealand met South Africa in their last preliminary match, in Perth on 1 February, Australia was left watching from the sidelines with fingers crossed.

The points system for the tournament incorporated bonus points, which in hindsight was not a satisfactory idea. A bonus point could be earned if sides won by scoring 25 per cent more than the opposition or won within 40 overs when batting second.

The way it worked out, the worst result for Australia in Perth would be a massive win to South Africa, giving them not only points for the win, but the bonus point as well.

The New Zealanders weighed it up beforehand and obviously decided their best chance of making the final, if they couldn't beat South Africa, was to lose heavily. This would ensure South Africa qualified, and would mean Australia could claim the second spot only if they won their last match, against South Africa, and also took the bonus point.

I'm sure New Zealand would like to have won their final preliminary match, but it didn't work out. South Africa batted first and were quickly in strife at 35–4 before Jonty Rhodes (107 not out), Mark Boucher (58) and Shaun Pollock (69 not out off

SPORT

- BOXING: Page 82
- GOLF: Pages 76-77
- OLYMPICS: Pages 72-73

Fleming's cynical decision not to try leaves Australia on the edge, so . . .

BENSON and HEDGES

ARE WE SQUARE NOW?

PAGES 85, 87

Joseph Romanos Collection

LEAGUE: GALLOP'S BACKFLIP MAKES HIM NRL CEO FAVOURITE AGAIN PAGE 78

How the Sydney *Sun-Herald* reported the controversy.

34 balls) thrashed a ragged New Zealand attack. The South Africans eventually reached 270–5.

New Zealand tried for victory initially but, at 72–4 with Vincent, Astle, Adams and Fleming out, were in trouble.

Then the drama increased. It became obvious New Zealand had largely shut down their attempts to score quickly. In effect, they were conceding not only defeat to South Africa but also a bonus point. Styris, Harris, Nash, Parore and Vettori played very sedate innings in the circumstances and New Zealand eventually eased through to 203–8. They duly conceded the bonus point. This meant that with just the last preliminary match, South Africa v Australia, remaining, the points were: South Africa 18, New Zealand 17, Australia 15. Because New Zealand had had the better of Australia head-to-head in the preliminaries, Australia needed to beat South Africa so comprehensively in Perth the following day that they took a bonus point and lifted themselves to 18 on the table.

In the event, Australia's victory by 33 runs was not good enough for the bonus point, so they missed a place in their own finals, only the third time that had happened in 23 seasons.

The final points were: South Africa 18, New Zealand 17, Australia 17.

Fleming was criticised quite heavily in some quarters for not trying hard enough to win, or at least not trying harder to make the game close. Up in the commentary box, there were some comments from the Australian television men that weren't totally flattering towards the New Zealanders. Apart from their parochialism they had a major concern over Channel 9's ratings: a New Zealand-South Africa final would obviously send those numbers through the floor. It wasn't unanimous — some didn't blame Fleming for one second.

The Sydney *Sun-Herald* the following day devoted its entire back page to the incident. With headings of 'Fleming's cynical decision not to try leaves Australia on the edge, so . . .' and 'ARE WE SQUARE NOW?' and a photo of Trevor Chappell bowling the underarm delivery to Brian McKechnie, the newspaper attempted to equate Fleming's actions to those of Greg Chappell at Melbourne two decades earlier.

Inside, the newspaper's two cricket columnists, Peter Roebuck and Geoff Lawson, offered their views.

Roebuck wrote: 'What happened was nothing like the underarm incident. But it was akin to a jockey pulling up a horse in a race and teams have been turfed out of competitions for worse . . . What has happened isn't particularly savoury. It is a product of the rules and New Zealand play the game to the edges, just as Australia have done so often . . . Cricket's legitimacy has been brought into question these past few years. Players need to rise above such jiggery-pokery and see the tradition that lies beyond.'

Lawson felt that Fleming did not deserve the hot reception he received from angry Australians. 'The underarm action was clearly against the spirit of the game and it still hangs as a filthy shadow over Greg Chappell's leadership. Fleming's actions could in no way be considered a spiritless act and will soon be forgotten . . . Fleming and his troops have out-thought the Aussies all summer and this has been no different.'

Richard Boock in the *New Zealand Herald* was adamant that Fleming had made a grave error. He wrote: 'Fleming flouted one of the most serious laws in cricket, but seems set to escape scot-free. Not only was the New Zealand captain's order to lose the game against South Africa a flagrant breach of the opening principle of the

International Cricket Council's Code of Conduct, it also appeared to fly in the face of a section which deals with corruption.

'Part C, section 10 of the code recommends a life ban for any player or team official who, among other things, "was a party to contriving or attempting to contrive the result of any match".

'Fleming said afterwards that he deliberately conceded a bonus point to the South Africans in order to improve his team's chances of qualifying for the series finals. But in concentrating on the bonus point he had first to decide to throw the match completely.

'Comparisons have been made with Australia's go-slow at Manchester in the 1999 World Cup, but the reality is that Steve Waugh's actions were not nearly as serious. At the World Cup, Australia were comfortably beating the West Indies and although they decided to play defensively at the end, they still won, and therefore did little wrong.

'Fleming's actions effectively predetermined the result of a match before it had taken its course, and encouraged his team-mates to underperform. The code of conduct also recommends a life ban for any player who induces or encourages any other player not to perform on his merits.

'The other rule which Fleming appeared to contravene was the opening clause of the code, which reminds captains that they are responsible at all times for ensuring that play is conducted within the spirit of the game, as well as the laws.'

I thought writers like Boock were well off beam on this one and agreed with International Cricket Council (ICC) chairman Malcolm Gray's view that the tri-series format had left Fleming in an invidious position.

Fleming took the most sensible course of action. Under the rules of the competition, as framed by the Australians, New Zealand found themselves in a position to make life more difficult for the Australians, and took that opportunity.

Imagine how the Aussies would have scoffed at the New Zealand captain if he'd gone soft and let Australia back in and they'd gone on to eliminate New Zealand from a place in the final.

It was noticeable that while the Australian media — and Boock — caned Fleming, there was little such criticism from Stephen Waugh and the Australian team.

They probably reflected on that match at Manchester during the 1999 World Cup when they deliberately took longer than they needed to beat the West Indies. By doing so they went close to cutting New Zealand out of the semi-finals.

New Zealand didn't like that at the time, but had to grin and bear it. You play under the rules provided. The best solution is to win your matches. That way quirky rules don't become a factor.

On the night in between the two Perth matches, I dined in good company at the home of former South African great Barry Richards. Graeme Pollock and Mike Procter were there, along with Messrs Benaud, Greig, Healy, Taylor and Ian Chappell. Being the only Kiwi, I copped plenty because of New Zealand's tactics during the day. The whole time the South Africans were listening and finding the Aussie attitude amusing.

Procter and Pollock, both involved with the South African team, called me over at one point and made it quite clear South Africa would rather play us than Australia in the finals. It wouldn't take a brain surgeon to work that out, but it was very obvious to me that their first target would be to stop Australia getting three points — that would get us through. I must say it seemed from the commentary box that South Africa's sole focus for most of the match was not on winning, but on keeping close enough to Australia to deprive them of that bonus point.

In fact, when South Africa reached that situation, their team began celebrating. They'd achieved their primary goal. Only then did their batsmen engage in a flog at the end of their team's innings, to make the final margin relatively close. Really there wasn't much difference between the attitudes of South African captain Shaun Pollock and New Zealand's Fleming, but it was Fleming who copped all the criticism.

11. Sixes of the best from big-hitting Cairns

Lance lets loose at the Melbourne Cricket Ground

Most New Zealand cricket followers will know what they were doing when Lance Cairns smashed those six sixes against Australia at the MCG in 1983. I know where I was. Having been dumped from international duty, I was playing a quiet game of Shell Trophy cricket, Central Districts v Wellington, at the Basin. As I recall, I didn't have an especially memorable game — one catch and a duck, caught behind by Erv McSweeney off Grant Cederwall.

While we were quietly playing out time at the Basin, Lance was going mad at the MCG. His fantastic hitting obscured a disastrous New Zealand performance. It was the second final of the Benson & Hedges tournament and New Zealand, needing to win to keep the finals alive, took a pasting from Kim Hughes' Aussies, who made 302–8. New Zealand replied disastrously and were soon 44–6 — Turner, Wright, Howarth, Jeff Crowe, Coney and John Morrison back in the pavilion.

We, along with most New Zealanders watching, were about to reach for the 'off' button. But you were always a little reluctant to do so when the big man strode to the wicket, just in case something happened. And it did. Lance got stuck in. He didn't win the game, or nearly win it — we still lost by a whopping 149 runs. But in a few minutes he not only restored a little pride to the New Zealand effort but turned himself into a folk hero.

That 34 minutes of hitting by Lance changed the public perception of him. After that, he seemed to be regarded by the public as a huge hitter who also bowled handily, though we in the team knew he was a really fine in-swing bowler who could occasionally catch fire with the bat.

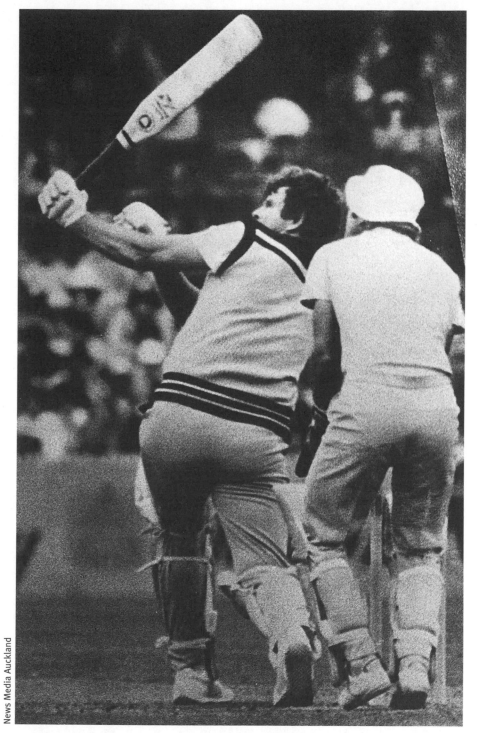

The birth of a cricket folk hero — Lance Cairns unveils his one-handed six-hitting

That day at the MCG, Lance reached his 50 off only 21 balls. On the way he carved six sixes. Here's a trivial pursuit question: who did he hit his sixes off?

He hit fast bowlers Rodney Hogg and the great Dennis Lillee for two sixes each, and meted out the same treatment to medium-pacer Ken Macleay. His most famous six was the one-handed swat off Lillee over Greg Chappell at square leg.

The non-striker during that bizarre period of play was Warren Lees, who often takes credit for 'guiding' Lance through. With the atmosphere and all the goings-on, it's doubtful Wally had too much to say or whether Lance in fact would've heard it anyway, as he was very hard of hearing. Lance made 52 that day and faced just 25 balls. Yet there can be no denying that in that short time he played one of the most famous innings in New Zealand cricket history.

It would be hard to estimate, but I would imagine that one innings meant a lot of income in New Zealand Cricket's coffers in the years that followed. Many fringe cricket followers joined the throng hoping they'd be there the day Lance Cairns did it again.

12. Power, pace and petulance

West Indies were at their worst in 1980

The West Indies team's visit to New Zealand in 1980 was probably the most controversial and incident-packed cricket tour ever to our shores.

I didn't see a lot of them up close and in person, though the little I did was enough to leave an indelible impression. I played for Central Districts against them in a one-day match at Pukekura Park. We made just 130. I made a duck, caught Greenidge bowled Roberts, and was one of four wickets to fall at 101. Desmond Haynes and Gordon Greenidge then knocked off the runs without losing a wicket.

Call it confidence or arrogance, but Lawrence Rowe, waiting to bat at No 3, never at any stage had his pads on and, before the winning runs were struck, many of their lineup were already back at the hotel.

They didn't appear the most friendly of opponents, but there was no doubting the ferocity of their much-vaunted pace attack. Andy Roberts, Joel Garner, Michael Holding, Colin Croft and Malcolm Marshall were a fearsome quintet of speedsters. They were fast and vicious. The West Indies' batting wasn't bad either. They'd toured Australia before arriving in New Zealand and Viv Richards didn't make the trip across the Tasman, but even so, Haynes, Greenidge, Rowe, Clive Lloyd, Larry Gomes, Collis King and Alvin Kallicharran formed a talented array of batsmen.

It was obvious just following the West Indies tour on television that they weren't enjoying themselves here. They probably didn't rate New Zealand very highly, and got increasingly irritated because they couldn't roll over us. They'd no doubt set themselves for the Australian segment of their tour — they thrashed the Aussies — and would have been expecting some easier matches in New Zealand. Instead they

Tempers flare as New Zealand scramble to victory in the first test at Dunedin. Gordon Greenidge (centre) kicks a stump out of the ground while Joel Garner (left) and Deryck Murray look disgusted. Umpire Fred Goodall confirms the match-winning leg bye.

encountered some 'sporting' wickets, some dodgy umpiring and a dogged home team determined to fight for every run and wicket.

The West Indians' behaviour on that 1980 tour was disgraceful. In hindsight, they got away with murder. Much of the responsibility must fall on their manager, Willie Rodriguez, and their captain, Clive Lloyd, but the standard of behaviour of many of their players was pathetic. They were very fortunate that the tour took place before the days of the Code of Conduct and International referees, because some of them would have copped hefty suspensions and fines.

There were many unsavoury incidents during the tour. The most notable occurred at Lancaster Park, during the second test. By this time, the West Indies were very grumpy. They'd lost the first test and were looking increasingly surly and unhappy.

After being bowled out for 228, the West Indies really launched into the New Zealand batsmen. Wright and Webb were out cheaply, Edgar had to leave the field injured and Howarth had his helmet knocked off. There was a lot of hostile short-pitched bowling.

But the New Zealanders fought hard and by tea were well in charge, with Howarth not out 99. Amazingly, the West Indies wouldn't come out after the tea break, apparently until umpire Fred Goodall was replaced. They'd gone on strike! Tension mounted and officials scurried about the place frantically.

Finally, 11 minutes late, the West Indies sauntered out. Howarth reached his century and the West Indies' effort slackened noticeably. They were jeered off the field at the end of the day. The next day was the rest day and word got out that the West Indies intended abandoning both the test and their tour. They removed their gear from the dressing room and Holding told some of the New Zealand players he would not play if the test did resume.

There were frantic phone calls to the West Indies Board of Control and meetings between West Indies and New Zealand officials in Christchurch. The West Indies eventually relented and play resumed on the fourth day. Richard Hadlee smashed a century, Jeremy Coney got to 80 and New Zealand totalled 460.

It was on the fourth day that the major incident of the test, and the tour, took place, one of the ugliest in the history of test cricket.

Colin Croft deliberately barged into umpire Goodall while delivering a ball. Goodall then had to walk the length of the pitch to speak to West Indies captain Clive Lloyd, who'd remained at first slip, arms folded.

I asked John Reid, New Zealand's long-serving international match referee, what he'd have done if he'd been on duty that day and he said: 'That was at the absolute top end of bad behaviour. Croft would have received the maximum penalty possible, including fines and suspensions. Clive Lloyd, the captain, would also have been in the gun, because of his failure to control his player or take action after the incident.'

Another outrageous incident from that tour occurred during the first test at Carisbrook when Michael Holding had an appeal against John Parker for caught behind turned down. Holding stretched out his follow-through so that it ended beside Parker, then kicked over two of the three stumps behind Parker. Again Lloyd ignored the incident and it was wicketkeeper Deryck Murray who tried to calm down Holding.

Here's what Reid had to say about this one: 'The merit or otherwise of the umpiring decision is irrelevant. Holding was guilty of bringing the game into disrepute and would certainly have been heavily fined and possibly suspended.'

In the years after that tour, various members of the West Indian team wrote books and they were always scathing about the New Zealand umpiring that season. Their attitude was that the umpiring was so bad they were pushed beyond normal human boundaries and that their reactions were only natural. Rodriguez, in one of his last comments before refusing to talk to New Zealand journalists any more, said: 'There is a limit to the physical and mental strains that can be endured.' New Zealand's cricket writers didn't see it that way, calling the West Indies childish and saying they couldn't take a beating.

The West Indies media at home totally supported its team. The Guyana *Chronicle* summarised: 'The deliberate design to defraud the West Indies team out of the series was so glaring that not even the Pope captaining a Vatican team would have taken it like a Christian. According to remarks made by the commentators during the broadcasts, it did sound like the umpires were cheating and they expect the docile West Indies to grin and bear it.'

> I'm sure there were some rough umpiring decisions, as there have been in every test series ever played. But the West Indians have never faced up to their unsportsmanlike behaviour. The quality of the umpiring was a red herring.

Several members of that team have gone on to relatively senior jobs in cricket. Michael Holding and Colin Croft went into the broadcasting commentary box and Clive Lloyd became an international match referee. I wonder how referee Lloyd would have dealt with Lloyd the captain.

There were many other ugly incidents during the tour. On the West Indies' way to a six-wicket loss to Wellington, Joel Garner had an appeal against Coney turned down. He glared, gestured and stalked about and informed acting captain Kallicharran he would not bowl again in the match.

There were repercussions felt for years afterwards. When we toured the West Indies in 1985, it was obviously payback time. The fast bowlers were consistently hostile, to the extent where Malcolm Marshall, one of the world's fastest bowlers, went around the wicket and fired ball after ball at tailender Ewen Chatfield's body. Jeremy Coney had an arm broken and most of the batsmen were hurt at some stage.

During one innings on that tour, Martin Crowe made an obvious attempt

Don Neely Collection

Stephen Boock grabs a souvenir stump and charges towards the pavilion and into the arms of delighted spectators after the heart-stopping one-wicket test win at Carisbrook.

to inform a local umpire that Garner was overstepping or no-balling by using his bat to remark the popping crease. Viv Richards raced up from slip in his role as captain and told Crowe 'to tidy up his own backyard' — an obvious reference to 1980 happenings. Interesting, considering Richards was not on that tour.

The West Indies returned to New Zealand in 1987, and still feelings lingered. Richards was still in charge. It was a torrid series and I think the West Indies were annoyed to come away from the series with only a 1–1 draw. They were certainly looking for more.

The pity of it all was that the 1980 season was historic for New Zealand. It marked the first time New Zealand had won a test series at home. In addition, New Zealand won the only one-day international in tremendously exciting circumstances.

The one-dayer was the first big game of the tour, and what a thriller it turned out to be. The West Indies made just 203–7. Except for Greenidge, who made a century, no batsman handled the bowling well. But New Zealand struggled too, and only some big hitting and gutsy fighting by Jeremy Coney (53 not out), Warren Lees (25) and Richard Hadlee (41) helped New Zealand get there with two balls and one wicket to spare. When No 11 Gary Troup went to the wicket to join Coney, the scores were level.

The test win came at Carisbrook when New Zealand, set 104 to win, got there with one wicket to spare, courtesy of a Stephen Boock leg-bye, surely the most valuable leg-bye in New Zealand history.

Chasing such a tiny target, New Zealand seemed well on their way at 40–2, but that was the thing about that West Indies team. They had tremendous firepower if they decided to use it. Holding, Croft and Garner bowled ferociously and not one New Zealand batsman got to 20. At 73–8, New Zealand looked gone. But then Lance Cairns and Troup took the score to 100. Finally Stephen Boock, not someone with great pretensions as a batsman, linked with Troup to add the final four runs amid excruciating tension.

In the second test at Christchurch, the West Indies again showed what they could do when the mood took them. They trailed on the first innings by 232 runs after their petulant, sulky display in the field. In their second innings, they put their heads down and treated Hadlee, Troup, Cairns, Coney and Boock with disdain. Greendige made 97, Haynes 123, Rowe 100 and King 100 not out.

13. When stats man Smith met glove man Smith

A tale of two Ians . . .

Ian Smith isn't exactly the most unusual name about. If you have a look in your local phone book, you'll see a lot more Ian Smiths than you will Daryl Tuffeys or Daniel Vettoris.

There have been four Smiths to have played cricket from New Zealand — Brun Smith, Dennis Smith, Syd Smith and yours truly. However, the cricket person I have most often been confused with was never a player of note. His name is also Ian Smith and he has been a fixture on the national cricket scene for 40 years, as a statistician and scorer supreme.

The New Zealand cricket community isn't especially large anyhow, but it was amazing how closely my path crossed with my namesake's. As a youngster, Kilbirnie Park was my favourite ground. I'd spend hours there watching the heroes of my youth, Barry Sinclair, Don Neely and the rest of the Kilbirnie senior team. Kilbirnie's scorer was Ian Smith.

As my interest in cricket grew, I progressed to a spell of manning the scoreboard at the Basin Reserve. In that capacity, I was extremely reliant on the scorers, who were stationed in the small box next to the scoreboard, on the eastern side of the Basin. The man who was a permanent fixture in that scorebox was, again, Ian Smith. He kept the score for Wellington for decades and was there, too, for the internationals.

Later when I progressed to first class and then international cricket, our paths continued to cross.

You'd think that now I am no longer a player, the grounds for confusion would have decreased, but it's been the opposite. Ian Smith, the statistician, has become

Ian Smith (left) and Ian Smith (right).

more prominent nationally because since 1983 he and Francis Payne have edited the *New Zealand Cricket Almanack*. In addition, Ian and Lynn McConnell wrote the *New Zealand Cricket Encyclopedia* in 1993.

His name crops up surprisingly often in cricket conversations. On occasion, I find myself being asked obscure statistical questions that I haven't a hope of answering. I sometimes receive letters from people wanting to discuss the *Cricket Almanack*. There is even more room for confusion nowadays because I work in the Sky television commentary box with Francis Payne. That means there is a Francis Payne-Ian Smith combination, and even more scope for misunderstanding.

14. All-round 'Tails'

A bit of luck . . . and a lot of talent

When Bruce Taylor made the test side in 1965, his team-mates called him 'Haystacks', reasoning that if he fell out of an aeroplane, he would probably land on a haystack. Later he became known as 'Tails', because of his surname. The connection with the toss of a coin, and perhaps some luck, seemed to fit.

There's no doubt about it: Taylor was a lucky cricketer. He made his Canterbury debut in 1965, when Dick Motz withdrew from the Auckland match with injury. He made the 1965 New Zealand touring team when Gary Bartlett failed a medical. And he made his test debut, at Calcutta, when Barry Sinclair withdrew ill just before the match.

But if the breaks went Taylor's way, no one could quibble with how he took his chances. He smacked 49 and took three wickets on his first-class debut, took five wickets in an innings the next week against Northern Districts and suddenly he was in the New Zealand touring side.

At Calcutta, Taylor made a slashing 105 and took 5–86 in India's first innings. He is still the only test player to score a century and take five wickets in an innings on debut. Taylor and Bert Sutcliffe, a left-hand batsman who employed somewhat more cultured methods, added 163 at faster than even pace at Calcutta.

Taylor was a really fine bowler. He was tall and had a high action. He moved the ball in the air and off the pitch and eventually took 111 test wickets, which for some years was the New Zealand record. In the West Indies in 1972, Taylor was overlooked for the first test, but in the next four he took 27 wickets at 17.46. On those wonderful batting strips and against a lineup that included such quality batsmen as Alvin Kallicharran, Lawrence Rowe, Roy Fredericks, Gary Sobers and Clive Lloyd, Taylor's bowling represents one of the best series performances ever by a New Zealand bowler, comparable even to Richard Hadlee's sensational 33 wickets in three tests against Australia in 1985.

As is often the way with fast bowlers, he is just as well remembered for his batting, and not just that debut test century against India either. I recall listening to the commentary of his amazing century against the West Indies at Eden Park in 1969. Taylor treated Sobers, West Hall, Lance Gibbs and the rest of them as if they were schoolboys that day. He reached his half-century in 30 minutes and in 86 minutes he slammed fast bowler Richard Edwards high over long on to bring up his century with a six. It is still the fifth fastest test century ever. He was out for 124, scored in just 111 minutes. He hit five sixes and 14 fours.

It's well-known that Tails suffered a personal tragedy in 1993 when he was forced to resign as a New Zealand selector after it became known he had stolen large sums of money from John McGlashan College, where he was the bursar. It transpired Taylor had become a compulsive gambler and that to feed his addiction he had resorted to theft.

It was a very sad fall from grace for someone who had provided cricket followers with so many golden memories and I'm pleased to say that Tails has fought back well. Since his release from jail, he has worked hard to get his life back on track and has become involved in cricket coaching in Wellington.

News Media Auckland

Bruce Taylor . . . never let a chance go by.

15. The long (or bent) arm of the law

Just when does throwing become bowling?

I'd love to have been a professional basketballer, but it was never to be. I'm 5 ft 8 in and my physical limitations meant that of all the sports that would be open to me, basketball was not one of them.

That's how I feel about Muttiah Muralitharan. The Sri Lankan off-spinner, who could in the not-too-distant future become test cricket's greatest wicket-taker, throws rather than bowls the ball. He sends down off-spinners and has a finger-spinner's accuracy. But because he jerks his arm, he gets a phenomenal amount of lift and spin, like a wrist-spinner. For Muralitharan, he gets the best of both worlds, accuracy plus lift and spin.

The ICC appears to have been quite weak in dealing with chuckers, as they're euphemistically known in cricket. For all sorts of reasons, various bowlers have been allowed to fashion long careers in top cricket, despite the fact that they do not deliver the ball in a legal fashion.

I've heard all about the Muralitharan defence: how he's had a deformity since birth and is therefore unable to straighten his right arm. If that's the case, then that's bad luck for Murali. But he's still breaking the laws of cricket and therefore should not be allowed to bowl.

It's amazing that he's had such a long career in international cricket and that on the rare occasions when he has been called, notably in Australia, it's the umpires rather than the bowler who have ended up copping most of the criticism.

The reason I'm a little sceptical of the birth deformity story anyway is that I have seen Murali bowl leg-spinners (when trying to complete an over after being

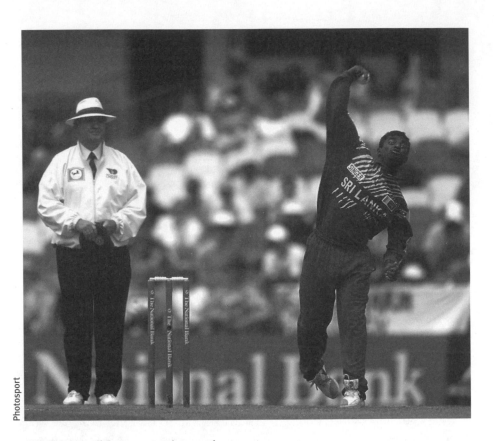

Muttiah Muralitharan . . . unique action.

no-balled) and he's bowled them very well. It is virtually impossible to bowl a leg-spinner with a bent arm. No bowler I can think of has ever been called when bowling leg-spin.

It's interesting to note that Murali has also forged a decent income playing county cricket for Lancashire. Yet the English have over the years taken the dimmest view of illegal bowling actions.

Sadly, I've personally never regarded Murali's achievements highly. He's not alone in biffing them. Pakistani speedster Shoaib Akhtar has a very dubious action. I'm not surprised many of the world's batsmen have questioned its legality, and I am surprised he has been cleared to continue. It must be almost impossible to pick up the ball when Akhtar slings one down at close to 160 km/h (100 mph). I have a suspicion Aussie quick bowler Brett Lee also throws some deliveries, especially when he's seeking extra pace.

There are one or two others about the scene. Generally they're the bowlers who deliver the ball with a chest-on action. It's a pity they're allowed to get away with breaking cricket's law, because in a way that penalises all bowlers who deliver the ball legitimately.

Chucking is not new. England left-arm spinner Tony Lock was a notorious darts thrower, until he was presented with incontrovertible evidence one day while touring New Zealand. The England team was having an evening at New Zealand captain John Reid's house in Wellington and some film that had been shot by Harry Cave (an avid taker of films) was being screened in the Reid lounge.

Lock was aghast to see the footage of himself bowling. It was as plain as day that he was throwing, and he resolved to sort out the problem, which he did. Harry Cave's film also exposed New Zealand fast bowler Gary Bartlett as having a definite kink in his delivery action, though Bartlett was never called in a match.

Geoff Cope, an Englishman who toured New Zealand in 1978, was another with a dubious action. Like Murali, Cope was an off-spinner. Their actions, though not within the laws, were entirely different.

There have been other celebrated cases, including Australian Ian Meckiff and South African Geoff Griffin. Sonny Ramadhin was known as a mystery bowler. He had a quick arm action and always bowled with his sleeves down, which helped disguise his delivery.

New Zealand has not been squeaky clean. In my playing days, I thought Michael Gill of Central Districts and Fred Beyeler of Wellington should have come in for a lot more attention from umpires than they did.

During the 2002 season, Jeremy Coney and I, while doing a television commentary, became increasingly concerned about the legitimacy of Kyle Mills' action. The Auckland pace bowler had just been named in the New Zealand team that was to tour Australia and I felt the way things stood the Aussie umpires might have a field day with him.

Jeremy and I had a look at some footage of Mills bowling, at normal pace and in slow motion, and were in no doubt that some deliveries were throws. The next day, while commentating on an Auckland game, we both said on air we felt Mills was throwing. We had a lot of film evidence to back up our charge. Better to have it pointed out by a couple of commentators in a domestic game in New Zealand than take him to Australia and have him exposed in an international arena.

There was no official reaction. I felt a few cricketers looking at us sideways for a while, but in the circumstances that was to be expected. As it transpired, Mills injured himself and was forced to withdraw from the New Zealand side.

16. Results you can't always bank on

The sad saga of match-fixing

Let me give a personal example of how the match-fixing scandal can envelop everyone who plays top cricket. It concerns my most memorable day in test cricket.

We were playing India in the third test at Eden Park in February 1990. On the first day, we found ourselves caught on a greenish wicket and were in big trouble at 85–6. It was not a lot better at 131–7 when I joined Richard Hadlee. Richard blazed his way to 87 and we put on 103 at faster than a run a minute. Once Richard departed, I stepped up a gear and I had a day when everything I tried came off.

Most batsmen will have experienced this at some stage in their careers. I was fortunate that my great day came in a test match when we were trying to get out of trouble. I eventually made 173 with 23 fours and three sixes. I am told it was the highest test score by a No 9 batsman and that at the time it was the fastest 150 in test cricket, as it came from 118 balls.

By the end of a madcap first day we had recovered from our precarious position and were 387–9. We went on to draw the match comfortably, and to win the series 1–0. I was very proud of that innings and have reflected fondly on it many times since — but just of late I've had the odd nasty thought that maybe it was not all owing to my skill.

Now we move on to the match-fixing scandals that rocked world cricket over the past decade. Two Indians have subsequently been banned from cricket for their part in the scandal, Mohammad Azharuddin and Manoj Prabakhar. A third, Kapil Dev, had the finger pointed at him by Prabakhar, but was subsequently cleared by the Anti-Corruption people.

Thinking back to that match at Eden Park, Azharuddin was the Indian captain and

I was overjoyed to score a test century against India at Eden Park. Now I have the odd flicker of doubt . . .

News Media Auckland

Hansie Cronje . . . at the time he seemed confident and capable; now when we look at photos of him, we see a cricketer haunted by self-doubt.

the opening bowlers were Kapil Dev and Prabakhar. I tell myself the Indians never stopped trying, that we made our runs on our merits. Or was it all too good to be true?

I mention the game to show just how insidious this match-fixing business can be. I suppose it's a back-handed insult to New Zealand cricket that we have never been implicated in any match-fixing scandals. Over the years, New Zealand teams have generally had enough trouble winning tests and one-day internationals on merit, without needing to be induced to lose.

With some countries, every time they have a bad result, the finger is pointed at them. Pakistan played poorly in their opening match of the 2002 ICC Champions Trophy tournament, losing to hosts Sri Lanka by eight wickets, and were immediately accused of chucking the game. Lord Condon and his match-fixing investigators were hot on the case, eventually deciding the Pakistanis had no case to answer.

That same week, New Zealand were thrashed by Australia by 164 runs and no one said a word. We bowled poorly, threw away wickets, misfielded and were sent packing in record fashion. Not a sniff of a match-fixing suggestion.

That's the trouble with match-fixing. It has happened, no question. But now the temptation is to look at every bad performance and ask whether it was as a result of accidental or deliberately poor cricket.

In my time as a test player, a span of more than a decade, the thought of throwing a match never crossed my mind. New Zealand teams I played in battled mighty hard for every success; no way would we have contemplated chucking matches. We were proud of any success we earned.

While New Zealand has not been in the thick of any match-fixing allegations — that honour belongs to South Africa, courtesy of Hansie Cronje, India and Pakistan — we have been touched by the scandal on occasion down the years.

Martin Crowe has been the New Zealand victim in all this. Several years ago, an Indian bookmaker named Mukesh Gupta fingered Martin among several well-known test players who had taken money for doing business with him. Other players incriminated included England's Alec Stewart, Brian Lara of the West Indies, Sri Lankans Arjuna Ranatunga and Aravinda de Silva, and Aussies Dean Jones and Mark Waugh.

Martin denied the suggestions of impropriety. He had, he said, taken some money in early 1992 for helping a man he thought was a journalist write about the World Cup. Once he realised the man was no journalist, Martin ceased contact with him. He was as surprised as anyone when that incident surfaced several years later and he found himself being mentioned in the same breath as Cronje as a match-fixer.

There was an investigation by New Zealand Cricket. Eventually, after a long time, Martin was cleared, as he had to be — he'd done nothing wrong. In instances like this, the accusation invariably gets much bigger headlines than the denial and the exoneration.

The whole business caused Martin a lot of distress. He does and always will hold a grudge against those who doubted him. To be honest, Martin outwardly coped with the sordid affair extremely well. I'm sure Lara, Stewart and the rest, who went through similar investigations, felt the same. Their word was doubted, their integrity questioned, because of the accusations of an Indian bookmaker of dubious standing.

In August 1999, New Zealand captain Stephen Fleming was approached by Indian sports promoter Ashim Khetrapal during the test series in England and offered a huge amount, said to be £300,000, if he could influence the result of the next test. Fleming and the New Zealand team management immediately reported the incident to the cricket authorities.

With all the talk about match-fixing, you can't help wondering about some results down the years. Three matches often mentioned involved New Zealand victories at home. On 16 March 1994, Pakistan and New Zealand met in the fifth and final match of the one-day series. At that point, Pakistan led 3–0 with one match having being tied. The fifth match, played in Christchurch, resulted in a staggering form reversal. Pakistan could manage just 145–9 in their 50 overs and New Zealand won by seven wickets with 16 overs to spare. The Pakistan cricket authorities launched an inquiry into the circumstances around this match. It was alleged Wasim Akram had offered young pace bowler Ata-ur-Rehman 200,000 rupees to bowl badly.

The inquiry never produced any concrete evidence of Pakistani players' shenanigans, but several of them were fined and one, Salim Malik, was suspended.

The pity of it was that the New Zealanders bowled very well that day. Danny Morrison had 3–20 off 10 overs, Chris Pringle 3–21, Gavin Larsen 1–21 and Chris Cairns 2–36. Those fine bowling figures now have an asterisk.

In 1995, New Zealand marked its centenary season in nightmare circumstances. After the forgettable tour of South Africa, New Zealand took on several teams at home in what was supposed to be a summer of celebration, and were roundly thumped. There was one bright moment. On 16 February 1995, New Zealand beat India at Napier by eight wickets. India were bowled out for 160 and New Zealand scored the runs in just 32 overs. At the time, the New Zealanders left Napier smiling. Then stories began floating back about India having thrown the game. Justice Chandrachud launched an inquiry in India (the results of which were not released for nearly three years, and led to no action being taken).

New Zealand captain Ken Rutherford seemed shattered when it was suggested the result had been fixed. 'It was about our only good performance,' he said. 'I'd like to think we did it on merit.'

During February 2001, New Zealand and Pakistan played five one-dayers. Going to Christchurch for the fourth match, Pakistan led the series 2–1. Pakistan played exceedingly poorly at Christchurch, and lost by 138 runs. Experienced pace bowlers Wasim Akram and Waqar Younis were very wayward, and the Pakistanis dropped some catches they should have caught.

Again the conspiracy theorists were out in force. How could Pakistan have played so badly? Ammunition was provided when the Pakistanis got back home and their coach, Javed Miandad, 'confessed' the game had been thrown. I didn't believe Javed. Knowing Javed, and what goes on in Pakistan cricket, I felt it was a tactical ploy on his part as he sought to shore up his position and that New Zealand had been caught up in it.

The most talked about game of recent times was the 1999 World Cup final at Lord's between, yes, Pakistan and Australia. Doubts were initially raised when Pakistan batted first after winning the toss on a cold, damp, murky London morning. All cricket common sense said that with their lethal pace bowling attack comprising Akram, Younis, Akhtar and company, fielding was the obvious option. They predictably failed with the bat, displaying some odd judgement and shot play.

Australia chased and overhauled easily a moderate total and became world champions, but even before the first champagne cork had popped questions were being asked and fingers pointed. It was mentioned that Pakistan had already suffered a shock defeat by Bangladesh in the tournament.

The final was one of the most classic cases of a side not using the conditions to their advantage when given an obvious opportunity. This in a World Cup final!

It seems these sorts of stories and accusations are never going to stop. It needs only one Hansie Cronje or Mohammad Azharuddin to taint everyone. That's the pity of it.

17. Seeing red and black

Dislike of Canterbury drove Blair to great deeds

Wellington's tearaway fast bowler of the 1950s, Bob Blair, compiled a magnificent record in Plunket Shield matches, especially on the Basin Reserve. He took 330 wickets for Wellington at an average of just 15.2 and at home was even more lethal.

Blair had some wonderful days, such as a haul of 8–36 against Central Districts, and another of 9–72 against Auckland. In just 59 games for his province, he took five wickets in an innings no less than 30 times and 10 times he took 10 wickets in a match. These are Hadlee-like figures.

But Blair always seemed to reserve his fiercest bowling for Canterbury. Year after year he made batting a nightmare for Canterbury's batsmen. In 1956–57 he had figures of 9–75 and 5–61 against them, destroying their lineup twice.

Blair had a thing about Canterbury. Christchurch was the headquarters of New Zealand cricket, and Blair felt he was always viewed unkindly at headquarters. He often missed selection for New Zealand teams, even though his figures were the best in the country, and he was regularly overlooked for the Winsor Cup as the country's best bowler in first-class cricket.

Bowling his best against Canterbury was his way of replying to these snubs.

'I borrowed a red and black Canterbury cap from Murray Chapple in my younger days,' said Blair. 'I kept that cap with me throughout my career. Before a net practice, I'd pin that cap to the back of the net, at about throat height. And then I'd be away, giving that cap hell!'

News Media Auckland

Bob Blair.

18. Worth Crowing about

Dad Dave's novel way of answering his coach

Dave Crowe was once told by his cricket coach at Christ's College, Derbyshire professional Les Townsend, that he would never make a test cricketer.

Crowe never did reach test level, though he played Plunket Shield cricket for Wellington and Canterbury in the 1950s. However, on meeting his old coach many years later, he was able to say: 'You were right — I made two of them!'

Dave and Audrey Crowe's sons, Jeff and Martin, not only batted for New Zealand, but captained their country as well.

Don Neely Collection

Proud father Dave Crowe with his sons Jeff (left) and Martin, who both captained New Zealand.

19. 'Umbrella' field ultimate in Aussie cheek

Nine man lineup provided Lillee ideal 'cover story'

Those Aussies were a cheeky lot back in the 1970s. Even though New Zealand beat them at Lancaster Park in 1974, it took them many years to acknowledge that we actually belonged on the same field as them at international level. They seemed to treat playing New Zealand as a good chance to get in some match practice before the challenge of real test cricket.

I'm pleased to say that that attitude has disappeared. Our successes against them through the 1980s altered that condescending attitude. It was very heartening, during the three-test series in Australia at the end of 2001, to see them scrambling to avoid defeat in the first test at Brisbane and again in the third test at Perth. Players like Nathan Astle, Lou Vincent and Shane Bond took the game to them and they didn't like it.

It showed that no matter how good a player is, he'll show strain under pressure and such class players as Mark and Steve Waugh, Shane Warne and Glenn McGrath did not play nearly as well when the New Zealanders took them on.

Dennis Lillee's cheeky umbrella field.

To give you an idea of how much things have changed, I think back to the two-test series in New Zealand in 1977. The first test, at Christchurch, was drawn after Ewen Chatfield and Dayle Hadlee had scrambled their team past the follow-on mark during a 10th wicket stand of 19 against Dennis Lillee, Gary Gilmour, Max Walker, Kerry O'Keeffe and company. In the second test, at Auckland, the Australians won by 10 wickets and Lillee took 11 wickets in the match.

During that series, there was the most extraordinary sight you'd see on the test field.

At Christchurch, New Zealand had to bat out the last 390 minutes and, assisted by an unbeaten century from Bevan Congdon, just managed to do so, finishing at 293–8. Congdon and Dayle Hadlee put on 33 for the ninth wicket.

Near the end of that partnership the Aussies — and let's not forget that the New Zealand team had just Chats to come — seemed to give up trying. With Lillee bowling, they placed all nine fieldsmen between wicketkeeper Rodney Marsh and point, the ultimate umbrella field. The bizarre field placing caused a bit of comment at the time, especially with the game so delicately poised.

The teams then moved north for the second test. In New Zealand's second innings, with a home defeat a certainty, Lillee was bowling at the tail. Chats, who hardly relished facing bowlers like Lillee at the best of times, was bemused, as he took guard, to see all the Australian fieldsmen swing over again to form a nine-strong slips cordon. Chatfield resisted Lillee and Peter Petherick was then dismissed at the other end.

But what had Lillee been doing? Was this an innovation in field placement? Hardly. Lillee was about to have a book published and was looking for a dramatic photo for the cover. He'd set it up in Christchurch, but no one had taken the picture, so he repeated the field-setting in Auckland.

20. Lure of cigars saw McGirr smoke Mailey

Herb was always happy to accept a challenge

Stan Brice and Herb McGirr were two of the key members of the champion Wellington Plunket Shield of the 1920s. Both were all-rounders who represented New Zealand and had long first-class careers. They were good mates who were constantly joking at each other's expense.

When Wellington played Otago in 1925, Brice was dismissed by Otago fast bowler George Dickinson when he mistimed a hook. The ball came off the edge of his bat, hit him on the head and Dickinson caught the rebound. Brice recovered consciousness in the pavilion and caused mirth when he said: 'I thought I was in heaven, for I found a parson [Blamires, the former Wellingtonian, then representing Otago], bending over me. Then I saw McGirr and knew I wasn't.'

McGirr, a vigorous, hard-hitting batsman and an accurate right-arm medium-pace bowler, thrived on a good battle, but also seemed to be a person who attracted colourful stories.

In 1924, when Wellington played New South Wales, champion Australian leg-spinner Arthur Mailey offered him a cigar for every six he hit. After debating with Mailey the quality of the cigars on offer, McGirr hit four balls out of the Basin Reserve on his way to a thrilling 92. One of them went through a window of the Caledonian Hotel in Adelaide Road.

The proprietor told the fieldsman retrieving the ball that he couldn't have it. She would deal only with McGirr. The game continued with another ball. When McGirr went to the hotel afterwards, the proprietor flung her arms around him and said the hit through her window was the best advertisement the hotel had ever had.

Herb McGirr . . . one of cricket's characters.

Though McGirr toured England with Tom Lowry's team in 1927, New Zealand's entry into test cricket came a little late for him and he played just two official tests before he retired. In those games, against England in 1930, he batted once and scored 51. He opened the bowling in both matches, but didn't have much joy, returning figures of 0–46, 1–65 and 0–4.

McGirr, always able to see the funny side of things, would have loved the fact that his test batting average put him in the elite 50-plus category, alongside names such as Dempster and Donnelly, and would have smiled, too, at a bowling average that placed him among the real part-timers.

21. Learning to survive on the tour of '55

Touring Pakistan has never been easy

In days gone by, touring India and Pakistan was riddled with as many stories of incredible conditions off the field as events on it. Indeed, in my experience as much time was spent putting together food and medical kits prior to tours as there was preparing in the nets.

I well recall the buckets of tears Jeremy Coney cried at Karachi airport when in 1984 the only bag that never turned up on our arrival from New Zealand was his personal food and treat supply. Or the panic on Evan Gray's face when he saw his chocolate-filled suitcase under severe pressure at Lahore airport, baking in the hot sun on the tarmac while he peered out helplessly from inside the aeroplane.

There are numerous memories of players armed with trusty bats standing on beds while rats were pursued around the 'luxurious' Bahawalpur guest house or queues 10-deep waiting to use the only microwave, arms laden with cans of Wattie's baked beans and spaghetti. So much more appealing to the players than the local menu.

There's also the instance of a rat being chased through the dressing room in Faisalabad only for the players to see it disappear down the only functional toilet. That proved to be the end of its sit-down use and I can assure you that clenching the cheeks for the duration of a five-day test in Pakistan requires grim and unwavering determination!

Bottled water always was regarded as liquid gold, tap water a no-no. Teeth were often cleaned in Coca-Cola or Fanta. All in all, if you got crook though, you were either careless or very unlucky, such were the standards and regulations set by the touring doctor.

Gordon Leggat has his turn in the team bath, Pakistan, 1955.

Touring even in the 1980s was an adventure. Mind you, what we went through on the Indian sub-continent was nothing compared to the suffering earlier New Zealand teams experienced.

The first time New Zealand toured Pakistan and India was in 1955–56 when Harry Cave led a team through an itinerary of 16 matches, eight of them tests. This must surely qualify as the most horrific tour ever undertaken by a New Zealand team.

Players speak of that tour as would survivors of famous battles like Passchendaele, Gallipoli or El Alamein. There are some famous images from that tour, none more graphic than that of Gordon Leggat, who wasn't nicknamed Tubby for nothing, with his ample frame squashed into a bucket that was serving as the team bath. That bucket was used by eight players who were crammed into one hotel room at Peshawar. As there were no washing facilities at the ground, it was the players' only opportunity to bathe.

Cave's team had to put up with primitive hotels, lack of hygiene, food poisoning, and serious disease and illness. And that was just off the field. On the field they had to contend with a relentlessly tough itinerary, matting wickets, intense heat and umpires too bad even to be called dubious.

Now and then modern players complain about administrators not understanding what they are going through. But at least recent New Zealand teams were never outfitted in heavy wool-based trousers and Viyella shirts as they embarked on a tour of one of the hottest cricket areas in the world.

Today players know what to expect when they tour that part of the world and, of course, conditions have improved markedly. There are now some world-class hotels, teams take a lot of their own food and videos, matting wickets have disappeared and one umpire in each international match is neutral. Back then, Cave's team had no idea what delights lay in store.

John Reid said the tour was 'one long tragic-comedy'. 'We usually had more players who were unfit than fit. Team selections were often meaningless because it was a case of counting the players who turned up at breakfast. If they were able to go to breakfast, they were selected.'

The New Zealanders returned home looking like they had endured lengthy spells in prisoner-of-war camps. Harry Cave, gaunt at the best of times, was now 12 kg lighter and virtually transparent. He had to miss some of the next series, against the West Indies, which cost him the test captaincy. Jack Alabaster was 79 kg when he left New Zealand and under 63 kg on his return. Bert Sutcliffe was so weak and sick that he was unable to play in the final two tests against the West Indies. He lost 10 kg and was a thin 63 kg when in the pink of health.

Fast bowler Johnny Hayes contracted hepatitis and, little more than a shell, went straight to hospital on his return, playing no more cricket that season. Tony MacGibbon contracted dengue fever and amoebic dysentery and has never really shaken off the effects. He lost 10 kg and, as he said: 'I didn't have a lot to come and go on in the first place.'

There were horror stories of players spending entire nights on a toilet. Matt Poore, who contracted a stomach infection early in the tour, spent several days fearing he would die and not knowing if that would be so bad. Alex Moir sat with him for three nights. One player, whose dysentery never really went away, batted wearing a towel tied as a three-cornered nappy.

The team had no doctor, or even a physio. Players took some time to understand all the local tricks. They were warned not to drink water unless it had been boiled, but didn't know that oranges, sold by weight, were soaked in water overnight to build up their moisture and weight.

Bert Sutcliffe said: 'We were guinea pigs in 1955. The only medication we had was

Matting wickets were another problem the New Zealanders encountered in Pakistan in 1955.

Halizone tablets, which you dropped into your carafe of water in the morning. The theory was that by night the water would be if not pure, then at least purer. Most of us would never have gone there if we'd known what it would be like.'

Reid recalled that while he was having a sprained ankle attended to in the pavilion at Bombay, he saw local officials preparing the iced water for the next drinks break. 'A huge block of ice was thrown on to the floor and then attacked with a hammer and smashed into pieces, then picked up and thrown into the water container. I'd seen rats scurrying around the floor.'

All these problems . . . and they hadn't even got onto the field! Matting wickets were set according to which team was batting. If New Zealand were batting, the wickets would be loose, meaning the bowlers got lots of assistance. If the locals were batting, the mats would be tightened.

Spectators would let off firecrackers or reflect the sun off mirrors at key moments when New Zealanders were batting. And if that didn't work, there was always the umpiring. In India the lbw count was 25–6 in favour of the home team. Worse, umpires had a finely honed ability to fire out key visiting batsmen who looked threatening while the rare successful lbw appeals against the locals were usually restricted to tail-enders.

The umpires could vary the tempo of their gait, from a trot if India or Pakistan were closing in on a win, to a barely discernible dawdle if New Zealand were on top and looking to press their advantage.

With other factors, such as an average of more than one official function a day, no replacement gear available, and the fact that India and Pakistan in 1955 could boast players of the calibre of Subhash Gupte, Vijay Mandrekar, Polly Unrigar, Pankaj Roy, Vinoo Mankad, Fazal Mahmood, Hanif Mohammad and Abdul Kardar, it's no wonder New Zealand struggled.

New Zealand teams have returned to this part of the world many times since. Each team has its own horror stories. The second New Zealand team to visit India and Pakistan was led by John Reid in 1965. They thought they'd made a huge advance because a doctor, Bill Treadwell, accompanied them.

Conditions have gradually improved and there is more awareness of what players are letting themselves in for. Even so, some players are extremely wary of travelling to that part of the world (quite apart from the security problems that have arisen over the past 15 years).

Richard Hadlee shied away from tours to the Indian sub-continent for some years and really returned only as he closed in on the world record for test wickets.

22. Otago the breeding ground for big scorers

Southern men rule when it comes to triple tons

Not many New Zealanders have scored a triple century in first-class cricket, but it's an undeniable fact that a player's chances of doing so are increased immeasurably if he comes from Otago. Just look at the statistics . . .

385	Bert Sutcliffe	Otago v Canterbury, Christchurch, 1952
355	Bert Sutcliffe	Otago v Auckland, Dunedin, 1949
338no	Roger Blunt	Otago v Canterbury, Christchurch, 1931
317	Ken Rutherford	NZ v DB Close's XI, Scarborough, 1986
311no	Glenn Turner	Worcestershire v Warwickshire, Worcester, 1983
306	Mark Richardson	NZ v Zimbabwe A, Kewkwe, 2000

That's it — the entire list of New Zealanders who have scored a triple-century in first-class cricket. Besides the three triple-centuries scored for Otago, Turner, Rutherford and Richardson were Otago players at the time of their big innings.

Do you notice the common thread? It seems that if you aren't an Otago player, you have no chance of reaching 300. Sutcliffe, Blunt, Turner and Richardson all played for other first-class provinces in New Zealand, but not at the time of their big innings.

This curious statistical fact has defied even great batsmen like Martin Crowe and John Reid during their world-record innings. Crowe was a Wellington player in 1991 when he and Andrew Jones shared in a mammoth partnership of 467 against Sri Lanka at the Basin Reserve. This was at the time a world record for the third wicket and a test record for any wicket.

Crowe, batting effortlessly, looked sure to reach the magic 300 as he stroked his way to 299. Then the Otago curse struck him and he was out, caught behind by Hashan Tillakaratne off Arjuna Ranatunga.

In 1963, John Reid smashed a world record of 15 sixes for Wellington while pulverising the Northern Districts bowling at the Basin Reserve. He was hitting so powerfully and scoring so fast that again 300 seemed assured, until he slightly mistimed an on-drive and was caught on the mid-wicket boundary by Gren Alabaster off Peter McGregor. Another couple of metres on that hit and he'd have had his 300. The next highest Wellington score that day was Paul Barton's 24.

News Media Auckland

Bert Sutcliffe . . . triple treat specialist.

While mentioning statistical oddities, how about this one, which has only been broken in recent years. Here's the list of New Zealand batsmen who have scored a century on test debut:

Jeff Mills   117 & 7 v England at Wellington, 1930
Bruce Taylor   105 & 0 v India at Calcutta, 1965
Rodney Redmond   107 & 56 v Pakistan at Auckland, 1973
Mark Greatbatch   11 & 107 not out v England at Auckland, 1988
Matthew Sinclair   214 v West Indies at Wellington, 1999
Lou Vincent   104 & 54 v Australia at Perth, 2001
Scott Styris   107 & 69 not out v West Indies at St George's, 2002

The remarkable thing about this list is that the first four batsmen listed are left-handers. New Zealand had been playing tests for 70 years and had played 276 tests before a right-hander — Sinclair — achieved the feat. At least he made a thorough job of it, becoming one of only four players to have scored a double-century on test debut.

Lou Vincent celebrates his century on debut for New Zealand against Australia in 2001.

23. MCG — the whole sad story

Famous stadium hardly a happy hunting ground for Kiwis

There's no doubt that the Melbourne Cricket Ground is one of the most impressive cricket stadiums in the world. On big occasions, with a huge crowd packed in, it has an atmosphere all its own. Boxing Day at the Basin Reserve has been great; Boxing Day at the MCG is unparalleled in cricketing terms.

Sadly, the MCG has not really been a happy hunting ground for New Zealand. That's not to say we have never done well there, but overall too many sad and bad things have happened to New Zealand cricket teams at the MCG for us to think of it warmly. I thought this was a relatively recent phenomenon until I began delving through the record books.

How's this for a catalogue of disasters and debacles:

17–21 February 1899. New Zealand's first visit to Australia, and to the MCG in particular. Against a Victorian team bolstered by six internationals, the game was a nightmare for New Zealand, who lost by an innings and 132 runs. New Zealand made 317 and 153. Victoria batted just once, making 602, with Peter McAlister totalling 224. Among the New Zealand bowlers, there were four centurions, Downes, Upham, Franikish and Reese — four of our best from that period. It was an inauspicious start to New Zealand's relationship with the MCG.

9–10 January 1914. Almost déja vu. New Zealand 141 and 188, Victoria 439. Victory to Victoria by an innings and 110 runs. Ted McDonald, Warwick Armstrong and other big names were way too good.

18–21 December 1925. Third time lucky? Not likely. New Zealand scrambled to an unimpressive draw. While New Zealand made 314 and 231–6, Victoria compiled

The famous Melbourne Cricket Ground, where so many New Zealand teams' hopes have foundered.

592–7 declared, with Stork Henry alone scoring 325.

12–16 November 1937. Victoria 141 and 293–5 beat New Zealand 210 and 223 by five wickets. Lindsay Hassett scored a match-winning 127 not out. Victoria fielded a team with nine internationals.

19–23 March 1954. Finally a bit of credibility. New Zealand 367 and 312, Victoria 423 and 108–4. The match was drawn, but is best recalled for the brilliant centuries of John Reid and Bert Sutcliffe. Just to be entirely honest, it should be pointed out this was a Victorian Second XI. The state's leading players were busy playing in the club finals at the time!

24–28 November 1967. New Zealand 298 and 161–5 scrambled a draw with Victoria, who made 402–6 declared, with Paul Sheahan 161. Once again we were outplayed by a state side.

Through the 1970s, New Zealand teams started to appear more frequently at the MCG. On New Year's Day 1970, New Zealand beat Victoria by six wickets in the V and G final, a limited-over competition contested by the states and New Zealand. The following week Victoria and New Zealand drew a first-class match. Victoria made 312 and 135, New Zealand replied with 220 and 94–3. The New Zealand batting was notable for the pair of ducks recorded by Glenn Turner and for the blazing 137 not out by Graham Vivian, the best innings of his career.

4 February 1972. More humiliation. The pride of New Zealand was thrashed by 76 runs by Victoria in the Coca-Cola (replacing V and G) semi-final.

Now we come to New Zealand's first test tour of Australia, in 1973.

On 30 November to 3 December, Victoria 262–7 declared and 324–8 declared drew with New Zealand 308 and 160–5. That was a warm-up to the test match four weeks later, the first time in 27 years that New Zealand and Australia had met in an official test.

New Zealand hopes were high. They were soon dashed. Australia 462–8 declared beat New Zealand 237 and 200 by an innings and 25 runs. Keith Stackpole made a century, Ian and Greg Chappell and Doug Walters half-centuries. The Australian media crowed after that. Ray Jordon, writing in the Melbourne *Truth*: 'Let's hope Australia disposes of them mercifully in the quickest possible time. Unfortunately the tour does nothing for cricket. The opposition is so feeble it provides no experience for our up and coming young players.'

There were a few more one-day outings — a loss in 1974, victory in 1975, and then nothing until the historic tour of Australia in 1980–81. Since then, New Zealand's matches at the MCG have involved some extremely controversial incidents.

Who could forget these?

Boxing Day, 1980. New Zealand turned up at the MCG for the third test, to be greeted by a huge banner designed by a local wag which said it all: 'All we want for Christmas is a five-day test' — this after we'd copped three-day test hidings at Brisbane and Perth. The team responded well and for once we had the Aussies on the back foot.

Jim Higgs, batting at No 11, was caught wicketkeeper Warren Lees, bowled Lance Cairns. Higgs had been batting 28 minutes before Cairns found the edge when he dug one in short. The only problem: umpire Robin Bailhache no-balled Cairns for intimidatory bowling. Geoff Howarth disputed the call and even Greg Chappell said later he disagreed with it. But Higgs and Doug Walters went on to add 60 for the 10th wicket and alter the complexion of the test.

1 February 1981. The infamous Underarm Game. Enough said on that. But don't forget the shameful disallowing of Martin Snedden's brilliant outfield catch of Greg Chappell. That decision swung the game Australia's way.

22 January 1983. More controversy. Greg Chappell wouldn't allow a substitute fieldsman for Glenn Turner and the umpires agreed with him. They claimed Turner had been injured before the game began. The result was that Turner had to hobble about for 12 overs before the New Zealand physio intervened and informed the umpires Turner's was a new injury.

13 February 1983. A big day for Lance Cairns, but another nightmare for New Zealand. Big Lance smashed his famous six sixes, but New Zealand lost the one-day final by an embarrassing 149 runs.

26–30 December 1987. Australian wicketkeeper Greg Dyer claimed a catch off Andrew Jones from what was clearly a bump ball during the third test. Jonesy was progressing well and had reached 40 when Dyer, to his eternal shame, claimed a fair catch when it wasn't. That piece of cheating subsequently cost Dyer his international career. From a keeping point of view, it is sometimes a little tough with the thickness of your gloves to tell whether a ball has definitely carried. These days it can be referred upstairs to the match official in the video room and often his view is non-determining. In Dyer's case he was caught red-handed scrambling for the ball, which was clearly carpeted. He had no defence.

Same match, last day. Australia, requiring 247 to win, stumbled to 227–9. McDermott and Michael Whitney, the No 10 and 11 batsmen, came together with five overs remaining. Richard Hadlee was on fire. He needed one wicket to claim outright the world record for test wickets. But it was Danny Morrison at the other end who should have had the crucial wicket. He had McDermott lbw, as any impartial observer would concede. The only problem was that umpire Dick French gave McDermott the benefit of whatever doubt he could find. To add insult to injury, Richard Hadlee bowled the final over to Whitney and, though he beat him everywhere, simply couldn't dismiss him. Australia were able to sneak away with a fortunate draw.

15 January 1991. New Zealand and Australia met in the second B and H Series final, at Melbourne. New Zealand struggled to reach 208–6, but fancied their chances

on a pitch offering plenty. Geoff Marsh was out first ball when Australia batted, caught behind off Richard Petrie. Two balls later Dean Jones, who at about this time was in his prime as a one-day batsman, was caught, but the appeal was disallowed. This would have left Australia sagging at 2–2. Instead Jones settled in and stroked a match-winning 76.

11 January 2002. New Zealand opened the VB series with a 23-run win over Australia. However, the gloss was taken off the occasion by a crowd disturbance that caused an eight-minute delay. About 200 spectators had to be evicted from the Great Southern Stand after hurling rubbish on to the field.

New Zealand captain Stephen Fleming said later he was concerned for his players' safety after a bottle was thrown near Mark Richardson while he was fielding in front of the unruly section in the old Bay 13 area. Fleming called for zero tolerance for spectators who behave badly. 'You can't put people in that position. We're there to entertain, not to be spat at and have stuff thrown at us, and we're not going to take it,' he said. 'It's not worth that much. It's not worth a guy getting a bottle in the back of the head.' Twice during the New Zealand innings, play was halted by ground invasions, but it was the incident involving Richardson that caused most concern.

In pointing out this incident, I'm very conscious that this type of occurrence is not limited to the MCG and our backyard is far from squeaky clean.

29 January 2002. Looking to sew up a place in the VB Series finals, New Zealand seemed to have Australia dead and buried. New Zealand made 245–8 and in reply Australia were 82–6 in the 22nd over. But Michael Bevan hit an undefeated 102 at faster than a run a ball and was supported by Shane Warne, Brett Lee and Andy Bichel and Australia got there by two wickets with three balls to spare. It was a game New Zealand should never have lost, but after what had gone on at the MCG over the previous century, should we have been surprised?

Footnote: perhaps it's worth noting that on New Zealand's finest tour of Australia, in 1986, when we won the test series 2–1, the three games were played at Brisbane, Sydney and Perth. Perhaps the reason we did so well was that we bypassed Melbourne!

24. When is a double not a double?

Kirsty Flavell a curious omission at 200 Club launch

The 200 Club was launched at a most enjoyable function at what was then Wellington's Park Royal Hotel on 17 February 1998. The function was a focal point of Bryan Young's benefit-year celebrations and the 200 Club was a clever marketing ploy, aimed at highlighting the fact that Young was one of the elite few New Zealand batsmen to have scored 200 in a test match.

He'd joined the exclusive group by scoring 267 not out against Sri Lanka in Dunedin the previous season.

To help raise funds, and as a special way to celebrate the occasion, former New Zealand fast bowler and talented caricaturist Murray Webb was commissioned to sketch each member of the 200 Club. His drawings were put on one print, signed by the players in question, then sold. The limited edition sold quickly.

The 200 Club at the time comprised:

Martin Donnelly	206 v England, Lord's, 1949
Bert Sutcliffe	230 not out v India, Feroz, 1955
Graham Dowling	239 v India, Lancaster Park, 1968
Glenn Turner	223 v West Indies, Sabina Park, 1972
	259 v West Indies, Bourda 1972
Martin Crowe	299 v Sri Lanka, Basin Reserve, 1991
Bryan Young	267 not out v Sri Lanka, Carisbrook, 1997

There was, however, one omission to the 200 Club print. There was no sketch of

Kirsty Flavell, who scored 204 against England at Scarborough in 1996.

The omission was picked up by many of the guests present and, besides the official limited edition print, another item was in hot demand — a menu signed by every member of the 200 Club, Flavell included. (All right, I've stretched the story somewhat for the sake of a good yarn. It's true Flavell was not on the official print, but her great batting was recognised by her invitation to the function and in the speeches that evening.)

Of course, nothing stays the same. The 200 club has grown markedly, even since 1998.

Joining the elite few have been:

Matthew Sinclair	214 not out v West Indies, Basin Reserve, 1999
	204 not out v Pakistan, Lancaster Park, 2001
Nathan Astle	222 v England, Lancaster Park, 2002

(Yes, I know Lancaster Park is now Jade Stadium, but I grew up knowing the ground as Lancaster Park and have an attachment to the name!)

Incidentally, some really fine batsmen missed the 200 Club. Among them have been Stewie Dempster, Roger Blunt, John Reid (both of them), Bevan Congdon, John Wright and Andrew Jones. A double-century in a test is not to be sneezed at.

Joseph Romanos Collection

Six of the best . . . caricaturist Murray Webb's sketches of New Zealand's test double-centurions in 1998. The list has since grown, but even then, Kirsty Flavell's omission raised eyebrows.

25. Blasts from the sub-continental past

New Zealand tours wrecked by bombings

Bombs and civil unrest ruined three New Zealand cricket tours of the Indian sub-continent within 15 years. Two of the tours were terminated; the third should have been. It is quite extraordinary, though almost certainly nothing more than unfortunate coincidence, that New Zealand should suffer in this manner so much more than touring teams from any of the world's other cricket-playing nations.

What is revealing as we look over the three cases is the contrasting ways the incidents were handled by the New Zealand cricket authorities. When the first bomb went off, in Sri Lanka in 1987, everyone — players, officials, administrators back home — was stunned. This was so different to anything that they had dealt with previously.

The second bomb, again in Sri Lanka, this time in 1992, resulted in chaos as New Zealand Cricket Council chairman Peter McDermott determined that one way or another the tour would continue. The fallout from this explosion was still being felt years later.

By the time the third bomb was detonated, in Pakistan in 2002, the situation was not novel and New Zealand Cricket Chief Executive Martin Snedden handled the appalling situation with urgency and common sense.

I was a member of the 1987 team. We'd played a warm-up first-class match, and the first test in Colombo when the tour was called off. In the late afternoon of 21 April 1987, a bomb exploded about 600 metres from our hotel, at a bus station in the centre of Colombo, killing more than 120 people. The whole political situation in Sri Lanka at the time was extremely delicate because of the domestic conflict between the

Tamils and the Sinhalese. Apparently 500 people had been killed within a week.

We questioned how we could live and continue to play cricket in such an environment. The first test had finished that afternoon and in the short time it took for us to get from the ground to the hotel, we found ourselves in the midst of a civil war.

A curfew was imposed in Colombo. The next day, a busload of 30 civilians was stopped on the road to Kandy, the venue for the second test, and butchered.

Over the next day or so, we had several meetings as a team and our management (Ken Deas, manager; Gren Alabaster, coach; Jeff Crowe, captain) consulted with the Sri Lankan authorities. The initial consensus within the team was strongly that the tour should be called off. One of the players' wives rang and said she didn't want to become a widow, and even some of the Sri Lankan players told us we should go home.

We had a special meeting with Gamini Dissanayake, a government official who was also the president of the Sri Lankan cricket board of control. He assured us we were not in danger, but some of us wondered how he could be emphatic about that when the evidence pointed to the contrary.

We realised that if we aborted the tour, it would be a financial disaster for Sri Lankan cricket and a sign that we had allowed terrorism to win.

After a number of meetings, discussions and open votes, a secret ballot came out 10–7 in favour of abandoning the tour, so our manager, Ken Deas, informed the New Zealand Cricket Council of our wishes and we headed home. Most of us were greatly relieved to leave the airport — and that came after an eerie bus trip through deserted streets late at night.

In a cricket sense, it was a great pity. Jeff Crowe had just been appointed New Zealand captain and, with Jeremy Coney retired and John Wright and Stephen Boock unavailable, younger players such as Andrew Jones, Phil Horne and Erv McSweeney were being given a chance to press their claims.

The first match, against a President's XI, was drawn, but was notable for the 8–81 John Bracewell took in the first innings. Braces came on in the ninth over of the innings and bowled 34 straight overs. Then we were into the test. Sri Lanka made 397–9 and when we batted, we had to fight hard in intense heat to hold them off. Jeff Crowe made 120 in just over 10 hours, one of the slowest test centuries on record, and Richard Hadlee batted nearly seven hours for a 151. They had taken our score from 160–5 to 406–5 when the match finished.

Late that afternoon, there was a real commotion both in and outside our hotel. Police cars and ambulances were racing around the streets, and staff and locals were talking in local dialect in a very excited and panicky fashion. That's when we ascertained that a massive bomb had exploded outside a busy bus station at peak time. I can assure you that peak time in Colombo means a lot of people. The bomber had chosen his moment well for maximum impact.

Photosport

Home, sweet home . . . shell-shocked New Zealand captain Stephen Fleming returns from the bomb-ruined tour of Pakistan, May 2002.

We were spared the sight of it because we were a distance away, but very graphic stories of absolute carnage quickly filtered through. It sounded sickening and soon thoughts for those affected, personal safety and returning home in one piece to families far outweighed the honour of playing cricket for our country. The telephone lines ran hot from our hotel back to New Zealand and some big bills were racked up as we reassured our families.

We were all a little stunned initially. We had been warned often enough of the possibility of this kind of event, read about it in the papers and seen from afar the odd snippet on television. But for it to happen just around the corner was mind-blowing.

Reacting to such events is a personal, individual thing. I quickly learned that people are influenced by horror and fear in different ways, but everybody's views should be respected.

The Crowes seemed to be especially unlucky in Sri Lanka. The next time a New Zealand team toured there was in 1992. This time Martin Crowe was the captain. The team had won a test series in Zimbabwe, then travelled across to Sri Lanka.

On 15 November 1992, a day after the team arrived in Colombo, history repeated itself. A motorcyclist, with a bomb attached to his waist, threw himself under a car carrying a naval commander and his three aides. The motorcyclist was one of the Tamil Tigers, assigned to assassinate the commander.

The incident happened only about 30 metres from the New Zealand team hotel, at about 8.30 a.m. The explosion was huge and sent pieces of glass, metal and concrete flying. There was chaos in the hotel foyer and when members of the New Zealand team got outside, they saw some horrific sights, including bodies without heads, separated body parts and blood everywhere.

A meeting was called by the New Zealand team management of Leif Dearsley, manager; Warren Lees, coach; and Martin Crowe, captain. The players, in various states ranging from shock to disbelief, generally wanted to return home, much as we had five years earlier. They felt unsafe, even after they were assured that this was an isolated incident, not part of an ongoing civil war. Manager Dearsley decided the team would meet again later in the day and told the players that whatever decision they reached, they would be supported by the New Zealand Cricket Council.

When that meeting was held, and a vote taken, it came out at 9–9 (besides the players, tour officials and, for some unexplained reason, Dearsley's wife Denise had a vote). It was obvious that too many players wanted to go home for the tour to continue.

The precedent had been set five years earlier and this incident was much more chilling because it occurred so near the hotel.

Players had been talking to their families back home. Pictures of the after-effects of the blast were being shown in New Zealand and naturally the families were very worried. Warren Lees spoke movingly of having his young son say down the phone,

'Daddy, you're not going to die, are you?'

However, other factors came into play. The Sri Lankans were desperate for the tour to continue. A major tourism summit was about to be held in Sri Lanka and having an international sports tour abandoned because of a bomb blast would be the last thing they wanted. Further, New Zealand Cricket stood to lose a considerable amount of money if the tour did not proceed.

So charging into battle went New Zealand Cricket Council chairman Peter McDermott, who was adamant the tour would proceed. Players who had spent a couple of days talking among themselves and waiting to be booked back to New Zealand were now forced to meet McDermott, first as a group, and then individually. McDermott imposed pressure on the players. He cajoled, begged, bullied. He offered contracts, spoke of their future with the New Zealand team.

In hindsight, the tour should have been called off. The players were in no fit state to play international cricket. They had already voted to come home.

But after McDermott's virtuoso performance, some of them, such as Ken Rutherford and Chris Harris, changed their minds. Mark Greatbatch, Gavin Larsen, Rod Latham, Dipak Patel and Willie Watson returned home, as did Lees. They were replaced by Grant Bradburn, Michael Owens, Justin Vaughan and John Wright.

New Zealand lost the test series 1–0 and were then beaten in the one-day series. The results were not surprising. Not only had the team lost some valuable players, but after all the discussion and dissent, anguish and anxiety, the players had other things on their minds.

The fallout from this tour lasted for years. McDermott lost empathy with many of the leading players. After what he did in Sri Lanka, his standing with them was undermined. Lees was sacked as coach, replaced by Geoff Howarth. Lees is emphatic — and I agree with him — that he lost his job because he walked out of Sri Lanka. He was assured he would suffer no repercussions, but he did.

He'd done a good job as coach, guiding New Zealand to the World Cup semi-finals earlier that year. He'd established a good working relationship with his captain, Martin Crowe. There was no cricket reason to sack him, but he was sacked anyway. I don't think Wally will ever forgive or forget and it took New Zealand Cricket a while to recover. Howarth came in and the whole show fell apart because Geoffrey lacked the discipline, back-up and organisation to coach the New Zealand team and did not relate well to Martin Crowe and to some of the other leading players.

The effects of that bomb blast in 1992 continued to be felt until Steve Rixon took over as New Zealand coach in 1996 and a new era dawned for New Zealand cricket.

As bad as the situation was in 1992, it was dramatically worse when the bomb went off in Karachi on 8 May 2002 and forced New Zealand's tour of Pakistan to be abandoned. The bomb exploded alongside a navy bus parked next to the New Zealand team hotel. This was an extremely narrow shave for the New Zealand side. Once again,

New Zealand coach Denis Aberhart and captain Stephen Fleming try to make sense of it all on their return from the aborted tour of Pakistan.

a Crowe was involved — this time Jeff Crowe was the New Zealand team manager.

Players were just finishing breakfast at 7.50 a.m. and thinking about boarding the team bus on their way to the National Stadium to begin the second test. In fact, physiotherapist Dayle Shackel was already on the bus.

The explosion was enormous. Windows of the hotel were blown in and there was a vast amount of damage to the area surrounding the hotel. As in 1992, but on a bigger scale, body parts were scattered across a large area. Fourteen people, including 11 French defence technicians, were killed.

The players were forced to see things that cricketers should never have to see. In effect, they found themselves in the middle of a war zone. It was extremely lucky that, with the exception of Shackel's cut forearm, courtesy of a piece of flying glass, no cricketers suffered injuries.

Naturally, thoughts of starting the test disappeared. New Zealand Cricket Chief Executive Martin Snedden acted decisively. Within two hours of the blast, he had called off the tour. There was no thought of giving the players a few days off, then resuming, or asking them to play in other, less-dangerous parts of Pakistan. He had arrangements made for them to return home immediately and a day later they were home.

When he was asked about the financial implications of his decision, Martin said: 'Frankly, I don't care. The safety of the players and the team management is what's important.' This attitude contrasted starkly with McDermott's a decade earlier.

Anyone who witnessed Stephen Fleming's tearful press conference on arriving at Auckland airport would have no doubt of the effects of that bomb. Fleming was in shock. He is an intelligent person and a fine international cricketer. He is not a hardened soldier. He was traumatised as he spoke of his own feelings and those of his team-mates.

Snedden, who was with us in 1987, deserved congratulations for acting so quickly and with such compassion. Arrangements were made for players who felt they needed it to receive counselling. In the circumstances, it was remarkable that not long afterwards, the New Zealand team could travel to the West Indies and win a test series there for the first time.

But I was not surprised when some players — Craig McMillan, Brooke Walker and Matt Horne — elected to make themselves unavailable for the ICC Champions Trophy in Sri Lanka in September 2002. Anyone who has been through such a harrowing experience would understand their feelings entirely.

As I reflect on those three New Zealand tours, two to Sir Lanka, one to Pakistan, I can't help but consider how much the scene has changed. A security advisor travelled with the New Zealand team to Pakistan, an indication of the fraught state of international security. And after the May 2002 bomb in Karachi, Pakistan's immediate cricket future was thrown into jeopardy. It was forced to play its next few home series in nearby — and safer — countries.

I cannot imagine that cricketers will be bursting to get back to Pakistan for quite a while.

26. Be afraid, be very afraid!

Life was tough with Malcolm in the middle

I ran into some good fast bowlers during my career: Richard Hadlee, Dennis Lillee, Jeff Thomson, Imran Khan, Allan Donald, Wasim Akram, Waqar Younis, Bob Willis, Michael Holding, Joel Garner, Andy Roberts, Colin Croft and Courtney Walsh.

I'd like to say that I gave them all a fair bit of stick, but that wouldn't be entirely accurate. Now and then I connected and if I was having a good day, I connected a few times. Generally, though, the fast bowlers worried me.

And I've no doubt which bowler worried me the most — Malcolm Marshall of the West Indies. He wasn't as physically intimidating as the likes of Garner and Ambrose. But I always sensed he really didn't like the batsman.

He seemed to have a nasty streak, absolutely delighting in seeing batsmen taking evasive action, or looking twitchy. Even bowling to a real No 11 like Ewen Chatfield, he would come around the wicket so he could launch the ball at the batsman's body.

During our tour of the West Indies in 1985, Martin Crowe and I killed the second test at Guyana. It was a nice flat track. Martin made 188. I came in when we were 261–6, chasing 511, and got to 53. Martin and I put on 143. We drew that test, and I felt pretty pleased about it all.

Malcolm did dismiss me eventually, last ball before tea. As we were all walking off, me because I had to, the others for a break in play, Marshall came up behind Martin and me and promptly departed from the gentlemanly call of 'Well played' to an uncouth 'I'm going to kill you in Barbados!' Charming, but pretty typical of the West Indies, who were not getting things their own way against a side they thought they'd hammer. It was Viv Richards' first series at the helm.

Malcolm Marshall in full cry . . . he was mean, he was fast and he was frightening!

The next test, as it turned out, was at Barbados, where the wicket was a lot livelier, and Marshall got his own back. He had figures of 4–40 and 7–80 and, frankly, he was terrifying. I made 2 and 26 and was dismissed both times by Marshall. I thought he was going to kill me that day. Marshall had extreme pace, he exuded 'attitude' and he could make the ball swing in late. He hit me on the arm during my second innings and I thought for a time my arm was broken. It wasn't, but it is fair to say he made his mark.

In his book, he described me as the most scared person he ever bowled to, which wasn't very complimentary. But it might not have been too far from the truth at Barbados!

He figured his remark to me had been relayed through our dressing room and had sent ripples to some of the others in the squad. That wasn't the case, as most had their own personal confrontations to dwell on.

I would love to have had a rum or two with Malcolm over the years to talk about those times, but of course, sadly, he passed away very prematurely.

27. Where there's smoke, there's dopes

No highs in Paarl 'pot' scandal

It would be impossible to have a book about the outrageous moments in New Zealand cricket and not mention the dope-smoking episode in South Africa in 1994. I wasn't on the tour and have not been privy to the confidences of the leading protagonists in what became one of the biggest debacles of the sport in New Zealand, but I have picked up the gist of what went on.

It was a sad episode, and was handled badly all the way through. The result is that it left New Zealand team-mates not trusting each other, or New Zealand Cricket.

When we think of various grounds and cities throughout the cricket world, we recall them for particular incidents. Bangalore was where Richard Hadlee broke the world record for the most test wickets. Headingley was where we finally beat England in England for the first time. Karachi was where the bomb went off in 2002 just as the New Zealand team was about to head off for the second test against Pakistan.

Paarl, a smallish town just inland from Cape Town on South Africa's west coast, will be forever associated with the dope-smoking affair.

The New Zealand team's 1994–95 tour of South Africa was hardly a raging success. After winning the first test, the wheels fell off for New Zealand. They dipped out in the subsequent triangular one-day series, and then lost the last two tests. The captain, Ken Rutherford, was fined 75 per cent of his match fee in the last test, after showing dissent. The coach, Geoff Howarth, had his contract brought to an end. The manager, Mike Sandlant, lovely bloke and excellent servant of the game though he is, resigned on his return. On top of that there was disgruntlement and lack of harmony among senior players.

The notorious dope-smoking incident in South Africa in 1994 claimed plenty of victims. Neither New Zealand captain Ken Rutherford (left) nor New Zealand Cricket chairman Peter McDermott emerged with reputations enhanced.

It was possibly the lowest time for New Zealand cricket, a fact that was emphasised over the months that followed when Rutherford's team 'celebrated' New Zealand cricket's centenary season with a string of spectacular losses at home.

The season's nadir was reached in Paarl. Without needing to regurgitate every detail, some of the players were involved in dope smoking at a barbecue put on for them when the game against Boland was abandoned after one over of the second day because of a sub-standard pitch.

Shortly after came the infamous Christmas Eve party with the Sex, Drugs and Rock 'n' Roll theme. Footage of players dressed in drag and partying it up was beamed back to New Zealand. It looked like good fun at the time, but when the drugs story broke and the pictures were replayed, they took on a more sinister connotation.

Rutherford was appalled when he was told by two people that up to seven players and one of the players' partners had been involved in dope smoking, and wanted New Zealand Cricket chairman Peter McDermott informed. Sandlant and Howarth felt the matter could be handled in-house.

So each player was interviewed and asked if he'd been involved. Though it was clear quite a group had smoked dope, only three — Mathew Hart, aged 21, Stephen Fleming, 20, and Dion Nash, 22 — had the spine to own up. They were three of the youngest members of the touring party and were badly let down by older, more experienced team-mates who were more concerned with protecting themselves than telling the truth.

The three were each fined 500 Rand (about $200) and that was supposed to be the end of the matter, though it's a matter of record that the team discipline did not improve and the results predictably got worse.

When the team got home, things happened quickly. McDermott got a whiff of what had gone on in South Africa and decided to launch his own inquiry. In his book, *A Hell of a Way to Make a Living*, Ken Rutherford points the finger squarely at a senior player, a bowler, whom he said dobbed in the players, accusing him of going to New Zealand Cricket with his solicitor.

Rutherford wonders why this player, whom he tags The Rat, would do that, questioning whether the player himself had captaincy aspirations.

A few years later Danny Morrison released his autobiography, *Mad As I Wanna Be*. He said he was the player referred to by Rutherford. Morrison said he did go to McDermott with Martin Snedden, his solicitor, but did not name specific players. 'Ruds believed I had gone to McDermott to sing like a canary and dob my mates in,' said Morrison. 'Ruds didn't name me in his book, but he described a player called "the rat" and that was directed at me . . . He should have known me better than that, and it upset me that he didn't come to talk to a guy that had played with him for 10 years on the circuit to ask what the story was . . . Frankly he got it badly wrong.

'I now believe that whatever Ruds made out of his book, the bottom line is that he sold his soul, because he never came to the horse's mouth to find out why I'd gone to see McDermott with my lawyer . . . It's a shame because in 20 years' time when we're a couple of former players in a room together, I probably won't want to have a beer with him.'

Besides this split between Morrison, his captain and other senior team members, there was the matter of McDermott dealing with the dope smokers again. Nash, Fleming and Hart believed they'd already been punished and that the incident had been put behind them.

But McDermott, perhaps seeking to show who was the boss with a display of fist-clenching, revisited the whole affair, conducting his own interviews. Eventually the three were suspended for the following one-day series against the West Indies.

I thought this was terribly unfair. They were in effect punished twice for one crime and, worse, they were punished only because they had enough integrity to own up.

When Chris Pringle released his book, *Save The Last Ball For Me*, he confessed he, too, had been one of the dope smokers. He never admitted it at the time, though he was suspended for other lapses of discipline in South Africa and, in fact, hardly played for New Zealand again. Other players who smoked dope that day in Paarl have never confessed.

It must have been a very split and angst-ridden New Zealand dressing room at the time, with players too ashamed to make eye contact with some of their team-mates. No wonder New Zealand's results were so bad.

The strange, and pleasing, part about all this is that the three who confessed all went on to enjoy long careers in top cricket. Fleming has become the long-serving New Zealand captain and is now one of the most respected senior players in world cricket. Nash, before injury forced his retirement, was a world-class all-rounder known for his competitiveness and aggression. Hart has had a long career with Northern Districts and in 2002 was recalled to the New Zealand team for the tour of the West Indies.

The New Zealand public is not bereft of common sense. It was plain to see that, misguided though Nash, Fleming and Hart might have been that day in Paarl, they were essentially good cricketers and fine young men. Public sympathy was almost totally with them. People knew they were upright enough to own up while some of their team-mates lied.

They served their suspensions and then got down to the business of playing good cricket, while some of their more noted team-mates got tied up in personal rivalries and battles.

28. You're nicked and named

Faces behind those strange names

Nicknames have always been a particular fascination among sports teams. The derivation of some of them is quite complicated.

There are the obvious ones, of course. Charlie Boxshall was Boxie, Johnny Hayes was Haybags, Harry Cave was Caveman, Bruce Taylor was Tails, John Bracewell was Braces, Stephen Boock was Boocky, Matthew Horne is Hornet, Craig McMillan is Macca, Chris Harris, Harry. Then there are those where a name is twisted slightly. Bruce Edgar was Bootsie, Ken Rutherford was Ruds. I was Stockley (one of my middle names). Bruce Murray was Bags (his initials were BAG). Some nicknames became so common they were used instead of the official first name — hence Curly Page, Sonny Moloney and Jock Edwards (Milford, Denis and Graham respectively).

Some were more inventive. Here is just a smattering:

Jumbo — Robert Anderson (also the man responsible for many of the following)

Chill — Tony Blain (obvious reasons)

Rabbit — Bob Blair

Beagle — Grant Bradburn

Sixer — Stan Brice

Springer — Lance Cairns (he came from Spring Creek)

Kong — Bill Carson

Bull — Jack Cowie

Ferret — Fen Cresswell (he went in to bat after the rabbits)

Cranky — Ian Cromb

Chopper — Jeff Crowe

Hogan — Martin Crowe (one of his early television favourites was *Hogan's Heroes*)

Dog — Cliff Dickeson

Squib — Martin Donnelly

Donk — Stephen Fleming (ask yourself)

Paddy — Mark Greatbatch (the Australian rugby player of the late 1970s was Paddy Batch. Also Mark was removed from Eden Park one afternoon by the gendarmerie)

Paddles — Richard Hadlee (big feet)

Bones — Geoffrey Howarth

Jed — Andrew Jones

Hammer — Chris Kuggeleijn (likeness to television character Sledgehammer)

Honest Wal — Warren Lees

Tubby — Gordon Leggat (obvious reasons)

Wolf — Erv McSweeney

Horse — Jonathon Millmow (now of journalism fame)

Mystery — John Morrison

Starlight — Frank Mooney (he operated well at night)

Daffy — David O'Sullivan (Daffy Duck)

Dag — John Parker

Mav — Adam Parore (derived from maverick, as in Tom Cruise in *Top Gun*)

Pizzle — Peter Petherick

Rowdy — Rodney Redmond

Bogo — John R Reid

Boy — Ian Rutherford (when he wasn't Ruds)

Piggy — Scott Styris

Knob — Shane Thomson

Flip — Merv Wallace

Dad — Lindsay Weir (he lost his hair early, smoked a pipe and had a reserved manner)

Shake — John Wright (his method of ironing)

Derek — Bryan Young

Sir — Any West Indies fast bowler of the 80s

Two of my all-time favourites were Mantis for Jeremy Coney and Mer for Ewen Chatfield. Mantis was a perfect tag for Jeremy. He looked all arms and legs. His nickname became so well-known that he wrote under that name in his Sunday newspaper column and his autobiography was called *The Playing Mantis*.

Mer was an abbreviation of Farmer, the initial nickname bestowed on Chatfield. He was also called Chats and Charlie, as in tail-end Charlie, and, on occasion, the Naenae Express. I thought he suited Farmer. He disdained any of the city-slicker trappings and there was a genial, rustic quality about him and his cricket. Jeremy decided Farmer should be shorted to Mer and ensured the name stuck by referring to Mer at every opportunity — in his writing, in speeches, at press conferences.

Chopper (right) and Mystery (below).

News Media Auckland

News Media Auckland

29. Convenor with the frankest convictions

Frank Cameron — a man of pride and passion

Frank Cameron was a tough bugger. In my early years in the New Zealand team, he was the convenor of the national selection panel, and I think he was one of the people who helped instil in us a bit more of the uncompromising attitude that allowed us to compete better at test level. I always respected Frank, and not just because he was the person chiefly responsible for me being selected in the New Zealand team.

Most of the blokes had a run-in with Frank at some stage when he was in charge. Mine came on my first tour of Australia when, as an ambitious young lad, I informed the convenor one night in Newcastle that since I was not getting picked for tour matches early on (Warren Lees was the preferred option) I would be better off back home playing first-class cricket.

Frank insisted that no one could be better off than representing their country on or off the field, but between expletives did give me the option of sleeping on the idea of going home — and reporting back in the morning.

Common sense prevailed. I ended up getting plenty of opportunities on that tour because Lees suffered a couple of injuries. I never forgot that one-on-one session with Frank at the bar.

Frank, whether selector or player, took tremendous pride in the black cap. Seldom when picking sides did he give one away cheaply and when wearing it himself would have died for it.

I always recalled a story I'd been told about when he toured South Africa in John Reid's 1961–62 team. New Zealand was playing Rhodesia at Salisbury.

News Mecia Auckland

Frank Cameron . . . a brave cricketer and a selector with plenty of common sense.

(I suppose nowadays they'd be playing Zimbabwe at Harare, and it would regarded as a test match.) On the last afternoon, the match seemed headed for a draw, but Reid was concerned that his bowlers keep things tight.

He asked Cameron to bowl out the remaining overs from one end, for Frank was a tight fast-medium bowler of the Martin Snedden-Ewen Chatfield mould. Frank apparently just nodded and got on with the job, grinding his way through a long spell.

At the end of the game, Reid was in the changing room next to Frank and saw that his boots were running with blood. Only then did the captain learn that Cameron had that morning had an operation for piles. He must have been in agony bowling during the afternoon, but he buckled down and did the job his captain wanted, without a word of complaint.

At times he gave interesting team talks, especially focused on the quick bowling aspects of the game, but his most memorable message from a team point of view came at the end of an abbreviated one-day international at the Basin Reserve in 1982.

We had been embarrassed by Australia in front of a full house, humbled in just a few hours. Bob Vance, also a hard but fair man, had read us the riot act in his role of New Zealand Cricket Council Chairman. After he left, Frank took a short turn on his feet.

'If you keep playing like that I'm going to lose my job — but rest assured a lot of you will lose yours first! Now let's have a beer and forget it,' he said.

30. Chats — and those dramatic innings

A genuine No 11, but a brave one

For a player who was one of New Zealand's best pace bowlers and worst batsmen, Ewen Chatfield, surprisingly, is recalled as much for two dramatic innings he played as for all his great bowling feats.

Chats had no pretensions to batting and was the No 11 in any New Zealand test team he graced. He was about the hardest-working and most reliable bowler in the world and made a career out of bowling upwind, the perfect foil for Richard Hadlee. Chats played in 43 tests and took 123 wickets. That's quite apart from his brilliant bowling in one-day cricket.

But, as I say, his batting was another story. Through much of his career it was a statistical curiosity to see if his runs scored would outnumber his wickets taken. Eventually they did. He scored 180 test runs at an average of 8.57. Included in his 54 test innings were 33 not outs and two of them are famous.

The first came at Eden Park in February 1975 when New Zealand met Mike Denness' England team in the first test. Chats and Geoff Howarth made their test debuts in this match. England, trying to recover from the pounding they'd taken in Australia from Dennis Lillee and Jeff Thomson, had a run-feast, scoring 593–6. Denness made 181 and Keith Fletcher 216. New Zealand was outplayed. They made 326 in the first innings and, following on, were 140–9 in the second.

Geoff Howarth was joined by Chats, fresh from his first-innings duck. The pair survived until stumps, having lifted the total to 161–9. This was frustrating for the Englishmen, who had to sit out the rest day then come back to take one more wicket for an innings victory. But when play resumed, things didn't go England's way.

This is the delivery before Ewen Chatfield was smashed in the head by a bouncer from Peter Lever. No helmet or arm guard in those days and Chats looks anything but confident.

The players seek help when it's realised how badly injured Chatfield is. Only the quick action of MCC physiotherapist Bernard Thomas saved his life.

Chats, using rudimentary footwork and sparring at the ball, somehow not only survived an attack that comprised Geoff Arnold, Peter Lever, Tony Greig, Derek Underwood and Chris Old, but worked his way to 13 not out. At the other end, Howarth played some pleasant strokes on his way to an unbeaten 51.

After nearly an hour, with the Englishmen getting increasingly annoyed, fast bowler Lever came back. He bowled a bouncer to Chatfield (remember, this was in the pre-helmet days) and the ball cannoned from the edge of Chats' bat onto his head, knocking him unconscious. It was a sickening sight for it was obvious immediately that something major was wrong.

Chatfield's heart stopped beating. He swallowed his tongue and began turning blue and frothing. Only prompt and decisive action by MCC physiotherapist Bernard Thomas saved his life.

Though Chats seemed to recover from the incident well enough, his confidence against quick bowling — never high anyhow — took a jolt. And it took him a couple of years to regain his place in the test side, despite consistently good bowling for Wellington.

Chats copped several pepperings after resuming his test career, but the worst were definitely in the Caribbean in 1985. Malcolm Marshall, in particular, had no qualms about going around the wicket and bowling straight at his ribs and head from an awkward angle. As usual, Chats stood and took it, but it was a pretty callous thing to watch from the dressing room and the non-striker's end, and it created some ill feeling at times.

The second memorable Chatfield innings — and one with a happier ending than the near-tragedy at Eden Park — came at Dunedin in February 1985 when New Zealand beat Pakistan by two wickets. This was one of the most remarkable finishes in test cricket. Near the end, the tension was so extreme that spectators were afraid to move.

Pakistan, needing a win in the third test to tie the series, left New Zealand needing 278 to win. Except for Martin Crowe, who scored 84, our top-order made a botch of the run chase and we were 23–4. Crowe and Jeremy Coney then put on 157 for the fifth wicket and at 180–4 we seemed to be on target again. Then there was another collapse (IDS Smith caught Miandad, b Wasim 6) and we were 228–8 and in really big trouble.

It was worse even than it looked on paper because by then Lance Cairns was virtually out of the match. Lance, batting without a helmet, was felled by a bouncer from Wasim and had to be helped from the field. He was badly concussed and was in no state to resume batting, although he maintained he'd have gone out at the fall of the next wicket.

When Chats joined Jeremy Coney, we were in effect 228–9, still 50 runs short of victory. The Pakistanis were looking very cocky. There was still more than two hours to play and the 50 runs we needed seemed far too many, especially with Akram bowling with such hostility and Chats not exactly known for his relish of the quick stuff.

Then followed the most amazing partnership. Jeremy made no attempt to shield the strike. He continued to bat well, but Chats often found himself exposed to most of an over. In fact, Chats faced 84 balls of their 132-ball partnership. Wasim, who was warned by umpire Fred Goodall for intimidatory short-pitched bowling, gave him a going-over. This resulted in an argument between Goodall and Pakistan captain Javed Miandad. Umpires generally win those tiffs and, thinking back, Fred had a couple of good tests for us at the 'Brook.

Gradually Jeremy and Chats whittled away the target, picking up singles and occasionally more. Superstition runs high in cricket dressing rooms, especially when chasing targets. Players generally find a spot and stay there until it's all over one way or the other. Through tea, hardly a word was spoken. Could the unthinkable happen? It was an emotional and dramatic afternoon of cricket.

The final charge was highlighted by a classic Chatfield boundary through square leg. Finally at 4.46 p.m. Coney tucked away Tahir backward of square for two and we'd won. Jeremy finished on 111, and his was a wonderful innings. But Chats was the hero. His 21 not out said everything about guts and determination.

Afterwards he could hardly speak. He was white with tension and shaking noticeably. It was one of the bravest innings I've ever seen.

It's more often than not the unlikely happening in sport, the underdog getting up against all odds, which results in tears being shed. There were more than a few seeping from the eyes of big tough grown men in the old Carisbrook dressing room that afternoon.

The whole country took something special from that afternoon. Test wins were becoming more frequent and almost expected, but that partnership between two good Wellington mates — the Mantis and the Naenae Express — while Cairns, the hero from Spring Creek, lay spreadeagled on the dressing room floor, pads still strapped on but basically non compos mentis, was the story at the bottom of every celebratory pint.

Chatfield was a particular hero. He was unique to bat with. In fact, he was inspiring from the other end. Why? Because as with his bowling, he never gave up trying.

Incidentally, Cairnsy went to Dunedin Hospital for overnight observation and missed a massive party. He returned the next morning still obviously not 100 per cent and reported that a brain scan had revealed nothing. 'What, nothing at all?' questioned Coney. 'Nope, nothing at all,' replied Cairns. 'Not surprising,' Coney concluded. You see, you can be brave when you've just won a test.

31. Quickie stalled on 99!

How Gary Bartlett was denied a first-class century

Gary Bartlett is often cited as the fastest bowler in New Zealand cricket history. The fastest New Zealand bowlers of my time have been Richard Hadlee in his younger days and Shane Bond, and I'm told that George Dickinson, the quick bowler of the 1920s, was very slippery.

Bartlett was apparently really something when he burst into first-class and test cricket as a teenager. He even had class batsmen like Australians Bobby Simpson and Ian Craig looking tentative and gave New Zealand some real firepower. By the time I was old enough to take notice of these things, Bartlett was probably past his best, though I do recall him playing against India at Christchurch in 1968 and causing havoc by taking 6–38 in the second innings.

The reason he's in this book, though, isn't because of his bowling, but because of his batting, one innings in particular. It happened during the 1959–60 season, only Bartlett's second in first-class cricket.

Bartlett was a handy lower-order batsman, not a genuine all-rounder, but certainly no bunny with the bat.

In Central Districts' match against Auckland that season, Bartlett batted really well and seemed set for his maiden first-class century.

Gary Bartlett is recalled for his searingly fast bowling, but there's a good story about his batting, too.

He and CD captain Ian Colquhoun had added 133 in 99 minutes for the 10th wicket when Bartlett, on 99, pushed the ball away and called for the run that would give him his century. It was a comfortable enough single and it is easy to imagine how the young Bartlett felt as he scurried through to reach the magic three figures.

Unbeknown to him, though, there was all sorts of drama happening behind his back. Colquhoun responded to the call quickly enough but never did get to the other end. Halfway down the pitch he tore a leg muscle and crumpled on the wicket in agony. He attempted to cover the remaining metres in a sort of crawl, but never made it. Colquhoun was run out and Bartlett was left stranded on 99 not out. He never did make a first-class century.

32. The day Andrew Jones weally saw wed

Aussie press man cops a serve from Jonesy

When Andrew Jones finally broke into international cricket, just before his 27th birthday, he had critics scratching their heads because of his unorthodox and somewhat ungainly batting style.

Coaches will always tell a batsman not to jump into position and to keep his head as still as possible. Jonesy would leap back and across when on the back foot and often hit the ball while on the move. It was his own style, and it suited him very well — as final averages of 44.27 (in tests) and 35.69 (in one-day internationals) indicate — though it was not a technique a coach would video and advise youngsters to copy.

His pet hate in the field was opposition batsmen getting cheap runs off our bowlers — now that really made him grumpy.

Jonesy was an individual sort of character in lots of ways. At an airport he was often to be found by himself, reading a book or in earnest conversation with his two great mates, John Wright and Tony 'The Chill' Blain. He had a slight speech problem, not being able to pronounce his Rs properly. He'd turn an R into a W. So 'present' would become 'pwesent'.

Out in the middle, he was always fiercely determined. He had terrific concentration and was a great fighter. These tendencies were never better illustrated than during his first tour of Australia, under Jeff Crowe in 1987.

He started off with 84 not out in a one-dayer against Western Australia, but then fell for only 7 in the first-class match that followed against the same opponents. Against South Australia Jones batted a long time to make 65 and 26. Some of the Aussie media climbed into him, saying he didn't look like a batsman

Andrew Jones in action . . . 'Where's that Tewwy Bwindle now!'

and wasn't much chop at all. They felt it was a real weakness for New Zealand to have him at No 3.

Terry Brindle, the experienced cricket writer for *The Australian*, was most uncomplimentary. The criticism mounted after the first test at Brisbane when Jonesy made 4 and 45. Australia won the game by nine wickets and there was a superior tone to the Aussie media's comments. Again Jonesy copped it from them.

Then we were off to Adelaide for the second test. Jones was at his most resolute. He made 150 (run out) in seven and a half hours, putting on 128 with John Wright and 213 with Martin Crowe. At the end of his marathon innings, he began his long trek across the Adelaide Oval back to our dressing room, which is square on to the pitch.

All looked normal as he half-acknowledged a standing ovation, in typical 'Jonesy' fashion, walking straight up the pavilion steps.

Halfway up he turned right and beat a path which took him straight through the middle of the open-air press box.

'Tewwy Bwindle. Where's that f. . . Tewwy Bwindle now!' he demanded in a loud enough voice. Some of the press looked decidedly embarrassed. We couldn't hide our amusement.

What Brindle made of it God only knows, but it was the last time the Aussies poked fun at Jones. He made 64 in the second innings and his test career was well and truly under way. How the New Zealand selectors of today would crawl over broken glass to have the gutsy former Nelsonian batting at No 3.

33. Tyros on the international stage

Experience not always necessary in test selection

During the 2001–2 season, when Northern Districts pace bowler Ian Butler was rushed into the New Zealand team in his first season of big cricket and after only four first-class matches, I was asked if he'd set a record for rapid promotion into the national team.

Butler's rise was indeed quick, especially as he was called into both the one-day and test sides. He showed the pace and ability to suggest he might one day become a leading member of the New Zealand attack. But his was certainly not the quickest promotion. Johnny Beck, Jack Alabaster and Graham Vivian all made their first-class debuts while representing New Zealand, Vivian in a test match.

Wellington batsman Johnny Beck was 18 when he was selected to tour South Africa in 1952–53, on the basis of some raw talent, his brilliant outfielding and some brief but promising innings in a couple of non first-class trial games.

Beck's first-class debut thus came for New Zealand against Eastern Province at Port Elizabeth and he scored 5 and 0. He made his test debut in the infamous Ellis Park test, scoring 16 and 7. Though he scored 99 (run out) in the next test, and was in the New Zealand team that created history by beating the West Indies in 1956, he never really fulfilled his early promise.

Jack Alabaster was 25 when he toured Pakistan and India with the New Zealand team in 1955–56. Alabaster wasn't exactly an unknown, even if the Otago selectors had refused to select him year after year. He'd impressed at Brabin Cup level and played for New Zealand Colts and New Zealand Universities, as well taking a large number of wickets for Southland in various representative matches.

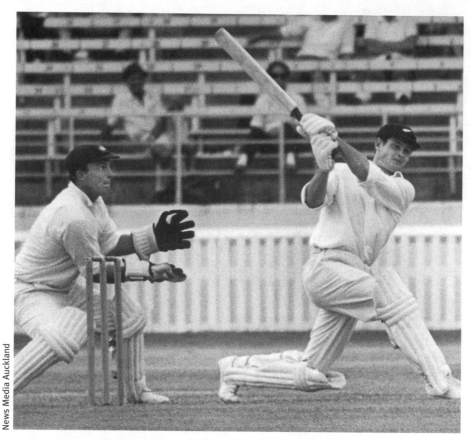

Graham Vivian . . . his first-class debut was also his test debut!

Playing on featherbed pitches against batsmen used to dealing with world-class spin bowling, Alabaster had a nightmare tour. In his first-class debut, for New Zealand against the Chief Commissioner's XI at Karachi, Alabaster took 0–32 and 0–39. This was apparently enough to get him into the test side, but in the first test against Pakistan he never bowled. Pakistan made 289 and Alex Moir, the team's other leg-spinner, bowled 37 overs.

Alabaster next played against the Governor-General's XI at Karachi, where he had 0–41 and 0–54. Thus on the Pakistan segment of the tour, he did not take a wicket. On to India, where against West Zone at Poona — five weeks into the tour — Alabaster finally took his first first-class wicket, on the way to figures of 2–8. This helped him regain his test spot, but still he could not take a wicket during 31 overs (0–96) as India smashed 498–4 declared at Hyderabad. With sickness rampant, the New Zealanders were by now looking for anyone who could stand up and Alabaster could, so he was in the side for the next test. Result: 0–83 off 25 overs.

Still he kept his test spot. In the third test, his 29 overs yielded a soul-destroying 0–90. It wasn't until the fourth test of the series that he got among the wickets, returning match figures of 2–60. Oddly, he was then dropped. Alabaster ended the tour with overall bowling figures of 19 wickets at 41.89. His test record was two wickets at 163.50. It was, by any stretch of the imagination, a rugged introduction to first-class cricket.

I'm pleased to say that Alabaster went on to become one of New Zealand's best spin bowlers. He finished his career with 49 test wickets and a total first-class haul of 500 wickets.

Another leg-spinner, Graham Vivian, had an even more rapid rise when he was chosen to tour India, Pakistan and England with John Reid's team in 1965. Vivian had just turned 19 when he was chosen. He was picked on the basis of his form in a net at Christchurch, after coming to the selectors' attention with his play for the Auckland Brabin Cup side.

Like Alabaster, Vivian found the going tough on his first tour. His first-class debut came in the second test of the tour, against India at Calcutta, and while he scored 43 (which was to be his highest test score), he took just 1–51 in the match. This was to be Vivian's only test wicket. He struggled for control and was not chosen again for a test on the long tour. In first-class games, his eight wickets cost 57.62 each.

Vivian was not destined to amount to much as a leg-spinner, but he did play quite a significant role in New Zealand cricket. He was a brilliant fieldsman — as good as anyone seen in one-day cricket today — and developed into an aggressive and brave left-handed batsman. He toured the West Indies in 1972 and eventually played in five test matches during his career, plus a number of one-day matches for New Zealand. For several years he captained Auckland with aggression and flair.

There must be a thing about leg-spinners. In 1927, the national selectors chose 18-year-old Cantabrian Bill Merritt for New Zealand's first tour of England after Merritt had had just one first-class outing, for Canterbury against Otago, when he had match figures of 8–68.

Merritt's selection for the 1927 tour proved to be inspired. Bowling day after day against the best players in England, he took 107 wickets in first-class games. On the following tour, in 1931, he took 99 wickets — a miscalculation that put him over 100 wickets meant he did not get a bowl in the second innings of the last game.

Unfortunately, the Merritt example might have done more harm than good because for years our national selectors would pluck out young players who'd played

Daniel Vettori . . . just 18 when he first represented New Zealand in a test match.

just a game or two at first-class level. Most were found wanting in test cricket.

The youngest players to represent New Zealand in tests have been spin bowlers Daniel Vettori (18 years, 10 days) and Douglas Freeman (18 years, 197 days). Both had just a couple of first-class games behind them. Vettori has gone on to be one of our greatest bowlers, but poor Freeman ran into Wally Hammond at his most majestic. He bowled while Hammond smashed a world-record 336 not out and might have been shell-shocked by the experience, for he hardly played again at first-class level.

In 1949, in-swing bowler Fen Cresswell was chosen for the tour of England after just one first-class match, a trial game. But Cresswell had been playing minor representative cricket for well over a decade and was 34 years of age.

I must say, in looking back over the careers of these youngsters chosen with so little big cricket behind them, that such selectorial gambles tend not to pay off. Every now and then a Martin Donnelly, Bert Sutcliffe, John Reid, Bruce Taylor, Vic Pollard, Craig McMillan and Daniel Vettori will come along — a young player who immediately looks at home at test level. But usually even outstanding players like Martin Crowe, Richard Hadlee, Bevan Congdon and Jeremy Coney need a bit of time to develop. If they've played for a while at provincial level, so much the better.

34. Snaring the great Don

Jack Cowie's once in a lifetime wicket

In the last 100 years or so virtually every great cricketer has played in New Zealand at some stage . . . with one notable exception. It remains a lasting pity that the incomparable Don Bradman never played in New Zealand. He was just a teenager and was non-travelling reserve for the strong 1928 Australian team's tour of New Zealand. The next official Australian team to visit New Zealand came in early 1946, but Bradman was at that point extremely ill and was unavailable for the star-studded Australian side.

There was one other occasion when Bradman might have played in New Zealand, and he came within a whisker of doing so. In September 1932 an unofficial Australian team, captained by Arthur Mailey, stopped briefly in Wellington on their return from a tour of North America. The team spent the afternoon giving a cricket exhibition at the Basin Reserve, despite the fact that their visit occurred in the heart of the local soccer season.

Bradman, however, did not play. Instead, he was driven over the Rimutakas to visit a stately house in the Wairarapa, and also gave an interview in the 2YA radio studios.

Though his first-class career spanned more than 20 years, he played against a New Zealand team only once, at Adelaide in November 1937. Curly Page's New Zealand team to England stopped off in Australia for three matches during their return journey and the first of these was against South Australia, captained by Bradman.

Jack Cowie, the New Zealand opening bowler, once described the occasion: 'We were all very excited because it was an opportunity to play against Bradman. We went and watched him having a net before our game and he was fantastic. It looked as if he was moving into position before the bowler had even let go the ball — that's how

Don Bradman pops into the 2YA studios in Wellington for a short interview, September 1932.

early he saw the ball and how quick his footwork was.

'The game began on a Friday and we batted first. We made only 151 and they began their innings an hour before stumps. We took a couple of quick wickets, and then in came Bradman. But he was obviously thinking about the next day. He was happy just to push the ball around for singles and made no effort to retain the strike. At stumps they were 64–2, Bradman on nine.

'The next day, Saturday, was supposed to be the day a big crowd would come in to watch Bradman bat. We were playing these games in Australia to recoup some of our tour expenses, so it was important we got a really good Saturday gate. We got to the ground about an hour before play, and Bradman was just finishing a net practice. I thought to myself, "Cowie, you're in for a long day today."

'I opened the bowling and the first ball was on a good length outside the off and Bradman edged it to Eric Tindill, who took the catch. It was a loud nick and there was quite a deflection. I shouted my head off, but the umpire took a very long time to raise his finger. I thought he wasn't going to give it. Of course, I was overjoyed to get rid of Bradman. Some of the boys said I'd cost us hundreds of pounds in gate receipts because thousands of people who'd been queuing up for entry heard Bradman was out and turned around and left. But I didn't care. I just wanted Bradman's wicket.'

35. Massacre at Ellis Park

Boxing Day 1953 — courage under South African fire

Of all the events in New Zealand cricket history, or in any country's cricket history, or even in all sports history, has there ever been a more dramatic occasion than what happened to the New Zealand team on Boxing Day 1953, during the second test, at Ellis Park?

The match took place in Johannesburg from 24–29 December 1953, and has often been referred to as the Boxing Day test. But this was a different sort of Boxing Day test to the festive, holiday tests we are used to seeing take place each year at the Melbourne Cricket Ground and, more latterly, at the Basin Reserve.

John Reid refers to the match as the Ellis Park Massacre, and that's in part the truth. Various members of the New Zealand team in that match have over the years given interviews, talking about what went on. They invariably become charged with emotion as their mind goes back to the events of that game.

Bert Sutcliffe and John Reid, two of New Zealand's most loyal and committed cricket servants, would have tears in their eyes as they discussed that day. Bob Blair, another of the principals, declined many interviews on the subject, saying it was 'too raw'.

However, he did, at Don Neely's request, do an interview with Joseph Romanos in 2001. It was the first and only interview he has given about that day. When I read the chapter on the Ellis Park match in Dick Brittenden's *Silver Fern on the Veldt* and when I think back to what it must have been like for the New Zealand team in that match, I can only shake my head.

New Zealand teams I was part of, I thought, had to endure some tough times,

Bert Sutcliffe collapses after being smashed on the head by a bouncer from Neil Adcock.

when conditions on and off the field were harsh and unpleasant. But nothing like what confronted the New Zealanders at Johannesburg.

Here is what happened. . .

The New Zealand team, captained by Geoff Rabone, went into the second test knowing they were up against a superior South African team, but determined to fight back after losing the first test by an innings.

Rabone lost the toss and South Africa batted all day on a difficult and green wicket. By stumps on the evening of 24 December South Africa were 259–8. Players from both teams were firm friends. They were staying at the same hotel and, as Jack Cheetham, the South African captain, said to Rabone before the tour, 'Our dressing room is your dressing room.'

The players left the field that day with thoughts of Christmas Day on their minds. There would be no play in the test. On Christmas Day, the New Zealanders celebrated with dinner at the Wanderers' Club where John Beck, the youngest member of the team, was elected to preside over festivities. Beck, just 19, was in the middle of his first test.

At the end of the day word filtered through to the New Zealand team of the terrible Tangiwai rail disaster back home, in which 151 people were killed. When the wall of Mt Ruapehu's crater lake collapsed, a lahar swept down the mountain into the river valley and washed away a railway bridge on the main trunk line near the township of Tangiwai. The Wellington to Auckland train crashed into the river below with huge loss of life.

Even more tragic news for the cricketers was to follow. In the pre-dawn hours of 26 December the day the test was to resume, New Zealand team manager Jack Kerr received a telegram informing him that among the dead was 19-year-old Wellingtonian Nerrissa Love, the fiancée of Bob Blair, the New Zealand team's 21-year-old fast bowler. The telegram had come from Blair's father.

Blair was sharing a room with Eric Dempster. 'At about 5.30 a.m. there was a knock on the door. Eric answered it,' Blair recalled. 'I could hear Eric and the manager talking quietly and phrases like, "I'll have to tell him" floated across to me. Then Jack gave me the terrible news.

'It's not a good experience when you are 21 years of age, and thousands of miles away from home, and it takes 28 days to get there by ship, to get that sort of news. No one should have to go through that. It was just a case of trying to cope with it.'

Word quickly filtered through the hotel, not only to the rest of the New Zealanders, but to the South Africans and the media, who were also staying there.

Blair did not go to breakfast that day. He remained in his room, utterly crestfallen. 'The rest of the team headed to the ground,' he said. 'Before they did, each one came into my room and offered his sympathies. There wasn't much they could say. I would never want anyone to have to go through that.'

So Blair stayed behind at the hotel with Jack Kerr, while the rest of the New Zealanders journeyed to Ellis Park. 'I followed the game a bit on the radio. There was no television back then,' said Blair. 'But really cricket was the last thing on my mind.'

At the ground, the New Zealanders discovered that the pitch, lively on the first day, had become a minefield, 'a snakepit', according to Reid. The last two South African wickets fell quickly and then it was New Zealand's turn to bat, chasing 271.

The South Africans had just the bowler to take advantage of the spiteful wicket, their 6 ft 5 in speedster Neil Adcock, who was not only extremely quick, but was a hostile bowler who was able to swing and cut the ball back into the batsman and extract considerable lift.

Rabone and Murray Chapple went out to open the New Zealand innings and had to face a fierce barrage. Both batsmen were hit repeatedly before Rabone was caught at slip. Shortly after, Chapple deflected an Adcock bouncer from his gloves into his chest and then on to the stumps. It was 9–2.

Just three balls later, Sutcliffe (a left-handed batsman) was struck behind the left ear by a bouncer from Adcock. 'I was going to hook it, but it came at me too quickly. At the last moment I thought I'd duck out of the way, but I didn't do a very good job,' said Sutcliffe. His ear lobe was split and he collapsed beside the wicket.

Rabone came back out to help his champion batsman get off the field. Cheetham approached Rabone: 'It's just plain bad batting, Geoff,' he said, intending to remove any suggestion that the South Africans were bowling at the body.

'I don't want to talk about it now,' said Rabone, 'I just want to get him to the pavilion.'

So Sutcliffe was carried off and taken to hospital for observation. He passed out twice more at the hospital. In came John Reid, to face a terrifying bombardment. Five times with successive deliveries he was stuck on the chest. There were several more blows before he was out caught for 3.

At the other end, it was even worse for Lawrie Miller, a left-hander who was a real front-foot player. Miller was pushing forward, as he always did, and taking a hammering. Finally he received a particularly violent blow in the chest and staggered from the field coughing blood. He, too, was taken to hospital.

Another Adcock bouncer hit Matt Poore and bounced onto the stumps. It was carnage. New Zealand were 35–4 with two batsmen in hospital.

In these circumstances out walked John Beck to play his first test innings. Has a new test batsman ever had to bat in a more calamitous situation? Beck and wicketkeeper Frank Mooney survived for 52 minutes, adding 22.

Their partnership was broken by the lunch adjournment, during which Rabone told the press Miller and Sutcliffe would not bat again.

But after lunch when Beck was out, for 16, Miller bravely returned to the crease to a loud ovation from the 23,000 who were at Ellis Park that day. 'There wasn't a lot said in the dressing room,' said Rabone, 'but I did advise Lawrie that he should not push forward. He needed to get on to the back foot on that wicket.'

Miller and Mooney added another 24 before Miller was bowled. At that point 41 runs were still required to avoid the follow-on.

By now Sutcliffe had returned from the hospital, where x-rays revealed no fractures. His head was swathed in bandages, making him look as if he was wearing a turban. He had a shot of whisky — a 'triple', as he recalled — then walked out to rejoin the battle.

Back at the hotel Blair listened to his team-mates suffering. 'I heard what was happening. The boys being carted off to the hospital one after the other, and I turned to Jack and said, 'C'mon, let's get down there.' The boys were struggling and it was no use sitting round. I might as well get down there and try to play some cricket.'

So Kerr and Blair caught a taxi to Ellis Park.

Sutcliffe was dropped at point by Hugh Tayfield, a simple catch, and then launched a glorious onslaught. 'I thought there was no point in mucking around. Might as well attack. It was probably a case of Dutch courage. The whisky must have helped,' he said. And attack he did. He hit the third ball he received over the square leg boundary for six and then twice in one over lofted off-spinner Tayfield for sixes. He and Mooney added 50 in just 39 minutes.

Finally Mooney was dismissed for a gutsy 35. Following him, Tony MacGibbon and Guy Overton both recorded ducks.

The dressing room at Ellis Park was far removed from the players' balcony. While the dressing room was on the ground floor, the players watched the cricket from the VIPs' tower, known as 'the Glasshouse', four storeys above. When Blair got back to the ground, he found the dressing room nearly empty.

New Zealand Cricket Museum

Bert Sutcliffe returns to battle, swathed in bandages.

'I got to the dressing room, found no one there, so got padded up and went out into the players' tunnel — it was really a rugby ground and this was the tunnel the players used to run onto the field. When Guy Overton was dismissed I walked on to the field.'

The effect was dramatic. Up in the tower the New Zealanders got up to leave at the fall of Overton's wicket. They assumed the innings was over as they had no way of knowing Blair had returned.

The crowd, which had sympathised with the New Zealanders during the brutal morning session and then cheered the smashing fightback by Sutcliffe, now fell silent. 'It wasn't good. There wasn't a murmur, not a murmur,' said Blair.

As the stricken figure of Blair made his towards the middle with 23,000 pairs of eyes watching him, there was not a sound to be heard. The spectators all knew of the tragedy that had befallen the New Zealanders, Blair in particular — the New Zealand flag at the ground was flying at half-mast and it had been announced that Blair would be taking no further part in the match.

Blair was obviously distressed. He brushed his eyes repeatedly, trying to wipe away tears with his gloves. Sutcliffe, blood seeping through his bandage, went out to meet his comrade, tears in his eyes too. Sutcliffe put his arm around Blair's shoulders and ushered him to the wicket, to the wrong end at first.

'I said: "What the hell are you doing here? This is no place for you. Look, we've already avoided the follow-on. Let's have a go and get out of here".'

The South Africans were just as moved as the New Zealanders watching. Roy McLean, fielding at square leg, said he had tears in his eyes as Blair walked past. 'I looked around our fieldsmen and they were all in the same state. It was the most dramatic moment I ever knew on a cricket field,' said McLean.

Blair saw out the rest of pace bowler David Ironside's over, playing and missing each ball by a considerable margin, and then watched as Sutcliffe took guard to Tayfield. There followed one of the most amazing overs in test cricket.

Sutcliffe pulled him over mid-wicket for six, lofted an on-drive into the crowd and, two balls later, repeated the shot. The crowd, especially the section housing the mixed race spectators, erupted. A single gave Blair just one ball (eight-ball overs in those days) to face. The spectators, already bubbling with excitement, went into a frenzy when Blair put his foot down the wicket and swung the ball into the far distance, way over the mid-wicket fence. 'There was a bit of anger in that shot,' said Blair.

'In all my years of cricket, I never heard a crowd make that sort of noise,' said Sutcliffe. 'When Bob hit that last six, it was as if a wave of emotion was released.'

The New Zealanders had taken 25 runs off the over. Sutcliffe smacked two fours in the next over, and then Blair was stumped. The pair had added 33 runs in 10 dizzy minutes, to lift New Zealand to 187 all out.

The New Zealanders left the field arms around each other's shoulders while the crowd rose and gave them an ear-splitting ovation, which was in such marked contrast to the deafening silence that had greeted Blair's arrival just a few minutes earlier.

'We got back to the dressing room, Sutty and me,' Blair recalled. 'He was my mate. I'm not a whisky drinker, but someone gave us a bottle of whisky and we got rid of most of it. We even took chairs into the shower and sat there drinking it. Sutty was in a state of shock and I was in a state of shock.

'It was a terrible scene in the dressing room. Most of the boys had been injured. They were spitting blood and I was almost crying blood. It's something that will stay with me for the rest of my life.'

It was not really a day for statistics, but Sutcliffe had scored 80 not out in 112 minutes. His innings contained only 28 scoring shots and his seven sixes was at that time bettered in test cricket only once, by Walter Hammond in 1933.

'Until Sutcliffe played it, such an innings existed only in the dreams of schoolboys,' wrote Denzil Batchelor.

'It was an amazing set of circumstances,' said Sutcliffe. 'It should never have happened. If Tayfield had taken that catch, which he would have 99 times out of 100, there'd have been no sixes. I'd never hit a succession of sixes like that before. It wasn't like me. I can't really explain what possessed me that day.'

The South Africans struggled to 35–3 at stumps, ending a day packed with sensation and bravery. The next morning the entire New Zealand team attended church together. They resumed the test, but had lost their desire and eventually South Africa won the match by 132 runs.

But as the *Cape Times* summarised: 'Memories of the match will not be of the runs made or of wickets taken, but of the courage displayed.'

36. Peter put Pakis in a spin

Petherick's hat-trick stands alone

Hat-tricks at any time are rare; at test level they should be savoured. After more than 70 years of playing test cricket, only one New Zealander has managed the feat — Peter Petherick, against Pakistan in 1976, and on his test debut at that.

Petherick's whole career was unusual and the circumstances of his hat-trick defy belief. It happened at Lahore. The New Zealand bowlers were getting slaughtered by Javed Miandad and Asif Iqbal, who had put on 281 runs in under four hours, when Petherick struck in his 16th over, by which time his bowling figures were a hardly fearsome 0–96.

First, he had Miandad caught by Richard Hadlee next to the square leg umpire for 163 after the batsman tried to pull one over the fence and instead got a top edge. Then he took a low caught-and-bowled to dismiss Wasim Raja first ball. As nothing out of the ordinary had happened in the test for about a day, this was really a frantic burst of activity.

In came Pakistan all-rounder Intikhab Alam to face the hat-trick. Fieldsmen, who moments earlier had been found in the far reaches of the Gaddafi Stadium, were brought in to hover around the bat. Petherick's first ball to Intikhab was on a good length. The batsman prodded forward, the ball popped up and Geoff Howarth at silly point dived forward to take a very good catch.

'When Intikhab came in I never really thought about the hat-trick,' said Petherick. 'The players were crowding around the bat. As I went back to my mark I thought to myself, 'If I was him I'd come down the wicket,' so I darted one in to him. He got a glove or hand to it and Geoff Howarth made a great catch. Everyone appealed and as

Geoff Howarth never took a more important catch. Intikhab Alam, c Howarth b Petherick. New Zealand's only test hat-trick.

I turned around to the umpire he was unmoved. I thought he wasn't going to give it, but then his finger went up. However, it was only after Intikhab had walked.'

Team-mates could not decide if the most amazing aspect of the hat-trick was the portly Petherick holding the return chance, or Intikhab walking.

Petherick, nicknamed Pizzle, was a popular and laconic character who was one of New Zealand's leading spinners when I entered first-class cricket. He came from Alexandra and for years took packets of wickets on the matting wickets of Central Otago. It wasn't until 1975, when he was 33, that he was picked for Otago.

He wasn't much of a fieldsman and could not really bat at all — in his full first-class career, he took 189 wickets and scored 198 runs! But he could bowl. In his first-class debut, against Canterbury at Carisbrook, he was bowling by 11.20 on the first morning and took the wickets of Coman, Hastings and Murray Parker — 3–39 off 16 overs. He also scored two not out, so right away the race was on between runs and wickets. In his fifth first-class match, he took 9–93 against Northern Districts, and suddenly he was in the New Zealand team.

Though he continued to take a lot of wickets for Otago, and Wellington after he moved there in 1978, he never played test cricket after 1977. Stephen Boock and John Bracewell came along and claimed the spin-bowling places in the test side. Bracewell was a good bat, and both were better in the field than Petherick. For a year or two, there was quite a tussle in the Wellington team for the No 10 batting position, Petherick eventually shading Ewen Chatfield for the honour.

37. A white wedding — in more ways than one

Eric Tindill's most unusual wedding day

Modern cricketers like to focus entirely on the forthcoming day's play during a test. Some will rise early, eat breakfast and have a stroll to relax. Others like to lie in for as long as possible. Their thoughts are centred around performing to the best of their ability in the test match.

It wasn't always like that. It has always amazed me when talking to cricketers of older generations that many of them used to go to work in the morning before heading to the ground to play for New Zealand. Walter Hadlee speaks of riding his bicycle to work to fit in some hours in the accountant's office where he worked, before biking to Lancaster Park to help New Zealand take on Errol Holmes' MCC team on March 6, 1936.

Work was still a priority into the 1950s. Fast bowler Bob Blair, describing his test debut, against South Africa in Wellington on 6 March 1953, said: 'I lived at Petone. On the first day of the game, I walked to the Petone Railway Station with my cricket gear and caught the train to the Wellington Railway Station. Then I walked to Whitcombe and Tombs, where I worked, until 10 a.m., before I went to the Basin to play South Africa.'

No one, though, was ever as busy as was wicketkeeper Eric Tindill on 27 March 1937, the final day of the New Zealand v MCC international at the Basin Reserve.

Here's how Eric described his day:

'I was married at 9 a.m. My wife Mary and I then went to town to have our photographs taken. In fact, we went to two studios because Crown Studios asked us to drop in there, too, so they could do a photo.

Eric Tindill . . . got married and saved a test on the same day.

'After the photos, we went back to Kilbirnie, for the wedding breakfast. There were some speeches, and then I had to rush to the Basin before 11 o'clock, because we were in the field.

'We struggled the whole match and they led us on the first innings by 162. We batted on the last afternoon and had to either bat until stumps, or score enough runs to make them bat again. We collapsed, except for Wally Hadlee, who made 82. I went in at No 7 and managed to stick around, but we kept losing wickets.

'Play was due to finish at 6 p.m., and we lost our ninth wicket at 5.30, when we were still behind their total. Jack Cowie came to the crease and we did our best to hang around. We pushed the odd run, but concentrated on playing safe. The clock moved very slowly.

'Finally, I looked up at the clock and it was five to six. We were about two behind their total. Then, all of a sudden, Jack snicked one to the boundary to put us in the lead. We were safe then because they didn't have time to start their innings. A moment later Jack was dismissed, but we'd saved the game by one run.'

There wasn't much time for celebration for Eric. A function for both teams was held at a hotel in Willis Street, but Eric was excused for a couple of hours so he could go home.

'I had to be back at the wharf by midnight because our boat, the *Arawa*, was leaving for England, taking our 1937 touring side.'

So there you are: Eric got married, attended to the formalities such as photographs and speeches, saved a test match, attended the after-match dinner, farewelled his wife and caught the boat to England, all on the same day.

38. Different strokes for different blokes

Golfing on the cricketing circuit

When New Zealand toured England in 1931, the team was taken to one of the exclusive golf courses near London. Not many of the team had played much golf and all-rounder Lindsay Weir was certainly no more than a novice. He began his round with possibly the two most stupendous holes ever played by a cricketer.

On the first he visited most of the surrounding trees, bushes and bunkers and eventually recorded a 20, which wouldn't have been too bad with the bat in his hands, but was less impressive on the golf course. However, any disappointment was soon put behind him because he achieved every golfer's dream, a hole in one, on the next hole.

'It was the biggest fluke you would ever see,' Lindsay recounted later. 'I hacked one out to mid-wicket, where it flew into a fence and rebounded towards the green. Then it hit the flagstick and dropped straight into the hole. A comedian couldn't have done the whole thing better!'

I suppose every team abroad will return with golf stories. One of my favourites concerns Lance Cairns in 1985. We were nearing the end of a torrid tour of the West Indies. Lance failed a fitness trial before the final test, at Barbados, so was confined to dressing room duties.

We were staying at the Rockley Resort Hotel, which had an inviting nine-hole golf course attached. Lance would attend to his duties at the ground, then head back to the hotel. As the days passed and his injury cleared up, he was able to get out on the course quite a bit. I remember one time he didn't exactly endear himself to us when we met him back at the hotel at the end of a particularly rugged day.

News Media Auckland

The bunker shots were good, but the putting caused problems. Golfer Lance Cairns in action.

'How did you go?' he inquired.

'Not bad,' we replied, 'except that we've got two in hospital and had another batting collapse. How about you?'

'Yes,' Lance said, 'I'm having my problems, too. I just can't seem to get my putting rhythm.'

39. When clothes don't quite maketh the man

Don Neely's day in the (painful) sun

I've known Don Neely since I was a young kid in shorts hanging around Kilbirnie Park. He was captain of the Kilbirnie club side and — of about equal importance in my eyes at the time — of Wellington, and was always ready to pass on a few tips to any boys keen enough to ask for help. Later Don became a Wellington and, for 14 years, a New Zealand selector. He was convenor of the national selection panel for seven years.

Don was a New Zealand selector throughout the time I was in the national team, so our paths crossed often. He has also been a prolific writer about cricket, as a columnist for newspapers and magazines, and, for 19 years, editor of the *New Zealand Cricket Annual*, compulsory reading for me. He's also written histories about Wellington cricket and the Basin Reserve, cricket-coaching books, and, most impressively, *Men in White*, the definitive history of New Zealand cricket.

So if I say Don is a cricket enthusiast, you'll understand it is a gross understatement. About the only thing Don never managed in cricket was to play for New Zealand. He was an aggressive but slightly rudimentary batsman, though by practice and determination he became good enough not only to play for Wellington, but to score a first-class century.

There was one day when he did get on the field for New Zealand, however. It's not easy to get Don to talk about it, but this is the story, as I understand it . . .

New Zealand was playing India at the Basin Reserve in February 1968. The match began on a Friday and New Zealand batted first. Don watched the day's play and then that evening had a convivial time of it with some cricket mates. Ever keen

Don Neely, who spent a never-to-be-forgotten afternoon fielding for New Zealand.

on cricket, Don arrived at the Basin in time for the start of play on Saturday, but was content to lie quietly on the western embankment in the sun while the New Zealand innings came to an end.

When New Zealand fielded, two or three of their players were suffering from illness or injury. Suddenly Neely heard the urgent tones of ground announcer David Grey hailing him over the loudspeaker. 'Would Don Neely report to the office immediately!' Grey commanded.

Don did as he was bid and was appraised of the situation. New Zealand was short of fieldsmen. His country needed him. So he was kitted out. He put on Keith Thomson's trousers, Barry Sinclair's spare pair of boots, someone else's large jersey, pulled down to cover the tie that was holding up his whites. Thomson, short and squat, was an entirely different body shape to Neely, while Sinclair, the shortest man in test cricket at the time, had feet several sizes smaller.

'I trotted out onto the field, in great pain because the boots were so tight, clutching the waistband to hold up the trousers,' said Don. 'Graham Dowling, the captain, sent me into the covers and I found myself trying to race after some drives through point while ensuring my trousers didn't fall down. I was terrified someone would sky a catch in my direction and there I would be circling under it, arms above my head, while my trousers fell down. I spent an uncomfortable half-hour or so on the field and was very relieved when one of the regulars returned and I could depart.

'People have told me it must have been an honour to field for New Zealand. Maybe it would have been under different circumstances, but that day it was an absolute nightmare!'

40. Putting my head on Butcher's block

The day I called for the captain's head

I've been very fortunate over the past few years to spend part of my New Zealand winters commentating cricket in England for Channel Four. It has been an extremely enjoyable experience, working with different and talented commentators and watching good-quality cricket at some of the world's most famous grounds. As someone said to me in jest one day: 'It beats working.'

Generally I've got on fine. I seem to have been well-received by the English viewers and my commentating style has fitted in well with Channel Four. There was a bit of a hiccup at the end of the 2002 season, though.

As the test series against India wound up, thoughts turned to the England team that would be travelling through Australia in 2002–3, trying to regain the Ashes. There was a time when the Ashes used to change hands regularly. As a lad, I recall listening to crackling radio broadcasts of Alan McGilvray, Lindsay Hassett and other commentators describing the feats of Ashes stars like Ray Illingworth, John Snow, Ian and Greg Chappell, Derek Underwood, John Edrich, Doug Walters, Dennis Lillee, Rod Marsh, Alan Knott and Jeff Thomson. The series were hard-fought and exciting.

But since the late 1980s — since the decline in the powers of Ian Botham, actually — the Ashes series have become very one-sided. Allan Border, Mark Taylor and Steve Waugh have led powerful Australian teams against England and, to be blunt, the England teams haven't really had a look in.

But you have to give the English one thing: they remain eternally optimistic. They always seem to feel that victory is just around the corner.

Anyway, we commentators at Channel Four were picking our England team for

Nasser Hussain offers advice to Matthew Hoggard. I created a storm by questioning his captaincy.

the Ashes tour. We all had much the same players, which wasn't surprising because really there was not a lot of choice. However, I threw in a bolter when I suggested that there should be a change in the captaincy. I opted to replace Nasser Hussain as skipper with Mark Butcher.

To say this was not a popular opinion would be to understate things. The English cricket community is very protective of Hussain. He is perceived as a gutsy battler, a good batsman, and a fine captain. I've no doubt he is worth his place in the side for his batting, but, having watched him captain England in New Zealand and in England, I have not been nearly as impressed with that aspect of his cricket.

I thought there was nothing to lose giving Butcher a go because to my mind, Hussain was going to struggle to match Steve Waugh in a battle of captains. Butcher has shown a good combative attitude and temperament in his international career and I thought he might be able to bring the same qualities to his captaincy.

The very suggestion of replacing Hussain provoked a storm, and I was left in no doubt about how misguided was my opinion.

On the subject of English cricket, I've often wondered why there are not more quality players produced in the country that not only invented the game, but which has, in the county championship, the most famous domestic cricket competition in the world.

I thought Lord MacLaurin of the ECB made a good point in 2002 when he noted that there were 480 professional players in the country. He suggested that it was impossible for England to sustain such a huge number of paid players. I agree with him. The system in England seems to put quantity ahead of quality.

There aren't nearly as many professional players in Australia, but they play a much tougher brand of cricket, and are far better prepared for the step up to the international arena.

Mark Butcher . . . I thought he deserved a shot at captaining England. What was there to lose?

41. Keepers who kept on keeping on

Boxshall and Rowntree were veteran glove men

Probably because I was a wicketkeeper myself, I have had a fascination with some of the men who kept wickets for New Zealand down the years.

Ken Wadsworth was an early hero. He really captured my imagination. With his blond flowing hair and his aggressive attitude, he looked like a player who thrived on test cricket.

He was a punishing batsman and an athletic wicketkeeper, and his early death was a tragedy for New Zealand cricket.

When you mix with former greats of cricket, as I've been lucky enough to do in commentary boxes around the world, you hear some genuine opinions, some of which don't go to air. To a man, the Aussies, including the Chappell brothers, Benaud and Co, always talk in glowing terms of Wadsworth. They respected him greatly as a tough, uncompromising cricketer and as a damn good bloke to have a pint with afterwards. In essence, he always gave as good as he got.

Turner's dual 100s in Christchurch to beat the Aussies were truly magnificent and match-winning, but who'll ever forget Wadworth's flowing cover drive to hit the final runs?

Another keeper, of an earlier era, whose name I took particular note of was Ken James. Besides touring England twice with New Zealand teams, he played for Wellington and, in the late 1930s, Northamptonshire. It was written that he formed an especially good partnership with leg-spinner Bill Merritt and certainly when I look at his victims, I can believe that.

In 204 first-class matches, he made 422 dismissals and no less than 112 of them

Walter Hammond is stumped by Ken James in England in 1931. One problem: the umpire ruled it not out.

were stumpings. That's a ratio of nearly 27 per cent, compared to the eight percent I achieved and Adam Parore's six per cent.

It shows how cricket has changed. I suspect batsmen were more inclined to use their feet and advance down the pitch before the Second World War, and wicketkeepers certainly stood up a lot more, even to pace bowlers. It also indicates he was probably far more adept at standing up to the wicket than either Adam or me. Messrs Bracewell, Boock, Patel and Vettori may well agree.

All of which brings me to Charlie Boxshall and Richard William Rowntree, the reasons for this item. They must be two of the most amazing characters in New Zealand cricket history. Both were born overseas, but served New Zealand with distinction in the game's early years here.

Boxshall was born in Melbourne in 1862, but played most of his cricket in New Zealand. He settled in Christchurch and made his Canterbury debut in 1898, at the mature age of 36. Soon after, he was picked for New Zealand, which was no surprise as critics of the time regarded him as one of the world's best keepers.

Despite his advancing years, Boxshall continued representing New Zealand until the First World War, by which time he was 51. He played his last game for Canterbury in his 53rd year.

I know some people like to joke that the wicketkeeper has an easy go of it, standing in one place for hours on end, but in all seriousness it can be incredibly taxing, squatting, sprinting and diving all day.

How Boxshall maintained his standards into his fifties defies belief. Incidentally,

The one and only Charlie Boxshall.

he returned to Australia after his playing days, and died in Sydney in 1924.

Rowntree was just as amazing. He was a Yorkshireman, born in 1884. At the age of 20 he began playing for the Yorkshire seconds and a county career beckoned, but he became seriously ill and emigrated to New Zealand, where it was hoped the clearer weather would help his health. It must have worked — he lived until 1968, when he was 84.

The reasons for my fascination with Rowntree are because he maintained his form until he was nearly 50, and because he stood up to all bowling. For Auckland, he stood up to Nessie Snedden, Mal Matheson and Jack Cowie, the fastest bowlers of his day. Once, playing for Grafton in a club match, he stumped New Zealand rep Rauol Garrard off Cowie down the leg side to earn victory for his team by two runs. Even Garrard applauded that one.

When he was in his late forties, he stood up to New Zealand opening bowler

Don Cleverley on a concrete pitch.

He continued to represent Auckland until 1931, when he was in his 48th year, and played senior cricket for several more seasons.

It's easy to overlook these old-time players, but Rowntree was obviously something special. Historian Tom Reese described him as 'a brilliant wicketkeeper, quite in the first flight'. Arthur Carman, the first editor of the *New Zealand Cricket Almanack*, wrote: 'He was unsurpassed as a stumper, especially to the bowling of Sid Smith. None could equal his certainty as he stood up to all bowling.' And Cowie, arguably New Zealand's second-best pace bowler ever (after Richard Hadlee), said: 'Dick was the best keeper I ever bowled to. It made such a difference having him standing up all the time, and he wasn't there just for show. He pulled off some amazing stumpings and could make the best batsmen jittery.'

Dick Rowntree must have been a character. Photos depict a short, squat, greying veteran with a sun-pounded, leathery skin. His hands were knotted and gnarled, the result of the flimsy gloves keepers worn in his day, more like the motorcycle gloves of today. He used to wear a large cauliflower leaf under his cap to cover the back of his neck on hot days.

While I'm on about wicketkeepers, just a word about two Wellington keepers. Eric Tindill kept for Wellington and New Zealand before and after the Second World War. Eric belongs to that select group of double All Blacks. He toured England with the All Blacks in 1935–36 and in 1937 with Curly Page's New Zealand cricket team.

Whenever he was asked, Eric would emphatically state that the cricket tour was immeasurably more demanding. 'I was the only keeper in 1937. Our manager, Tom Lowry, played a couple of games to give me a rest, but otherwise I did it six days a week for five months. We didn't play on Sundays back then, and I used to look forward to Sundays, I can tell you.'

Eric did say that the cricketers were 'well off' compared to the rugby players. 'With the All Blacks we received three shillings a day, and even then not in cash, but in vouchers that had to be spent at the hotel where we were staying. The cricketers got eight shillings a day and as we were playing all day, there wasn't as much chance to spend it!'

Perhaps today's New Zealand cricketers, with their threats of strikes and their disputes over contracts and salaries, should reflect on what players in Tindill's day regarded as well-paid.

Frank Mooney was the man who succeeded Tindill as the New Zealand team wicketkeeper. He was the main wicketkeeper in Walter Hadlee's 1949 team to England (John Reid was his part-time deputy) and kept in 27 matches. In them he made 65 dismissals, 44 caught and 21 stumped. That total was a record for a visiting keeper, exceeding even what Bert Oldfield managed on his four tours of England or the legendary Don Tallon's 43 victims in 1948.

42. A knight and his shining Alfa

Richard Hadlee — special player, special case

I feel very fortunate that my international career coincided with Richard Hadlee's. He is certainly one of the giants of New Zealand cricket and during the 1980s there were times when he was the best pace bowler in the world. When Richard began his New Zealand career, in 1972, we'd won seven tests. By the time he finished, in 1990, that number had increased to 29.

He finished his spectacular test career at Edgbaston, Birmingham in 1990 at the age of 39. Incidentally, Adam Parore, aged 19, was making his debut. Richard took a wicket with his last ball in test cricket, his 431st in all. The victim was Devon Malcolm, who honestly could not bat. If you ask Richard, though, he'll tell you it didn't matter. A test wicket is a test wicket — he was a stats man to the end.

Richard averaged five wickets a test throughout his 86 tests. But in the games we won, he averaged seven, which is a really remarkable strike rate.

It was very comforting having Richard in the team. It meant that even on the longest afternoons, or on the flattest wickets, against the best batsmen, we knew we had someone capable of taking wickets. A spell by Richard was like a bowling clinic: the run up silky, the pace slippery and the movement sideways of the pitch and in the air quite remarkable. As they say, he had it on a string.

I suppose the peak of his career was in Australia in 1985, when he took 33 wickets in the three-test series. He destroyed the Aussies that year, and not only in the first test, at Brisbane, when he had his famous 9–52 in the first innings. Having said that, he was a consistently brilliant bowler, as can be seen by the fact that from 1976–90 he won the Winsor Cup for the country's best bowler in first-class cricket every year but one. And that season, 1987–88, he missed a large amount of cricket through injury and still ran the eventual winner, Ewen Chatfield, close.

I won't go into all Hadlee's bowling feats. He's written several books himself, and there are books and videos about him. He was an amazing cricketer, though. Not only was he a great bowler, but he was such a good batsman that I believe he could have justified a place in the test side purely as a batsman if he had devoted himself to that part of the game. He made two test centuries and smashed a match-winning 99 against England at Christchurch in 1984. He was a consistently effective lower-order batsman in one-day cricket.

Though Richard was tall, he wasn't a hefty bloke in the Dick Motz-Lance Cairns-Chris Cairns mould. But he hit some massive sixes because of his sweet timing and clean hitting.

In the field, Richard was an agile outfielder and took some superb catches in the gully. No surprise that he was also a brilliant soccer goalkeeper and rose to a good level in that sport. He was in every sense a natural, but he worked hard at his game until by the 1980s he was the consummate professional. His spell with English county Notts was the making of him as a player and his partnership there with South African Clive Rice was more often than not the making of Notts.

Ironically, he is probably even more highly revered these days at Trent Bridge than he is back home. The new stand at the Radcliffe Road end is highlighted by Hadlee function rooms, waiting rooms and memorabilia. He is regarded as their very best and that's at a county that boasted the services of one Garfield Sobers.

He was really a once-in-a-lifetime cricketer. Certainly his pedigree was impeccable. His father, Walter, was one of our leading test batsmen of his time and a New Zealand captain. He was also a New Zealand selector, team manager and chairman of the board of the New Zealand Cricket Council. Richard's older brothers Barry and Dayle represented New Zealand. Dayle is now a top New Zealand coach and Richard is the chairman of national selectors. It's a pretty formidable family contribution.

Like most people who are genuinely outstanding, Richard had idiosyncrasies that set him apart. If I think of New Zealand's best players of the past 30 years — Glenn Turner, Martin Crowe, Richard Hadlee, Chris Cairns — they were all extremely individual in their approach.

Some of Richard's team-mates used to get annoyed with him, feeling that he regarded himself as a special case. I recall jogging around the Basin Reserve with the rest of the New Zealand team on the day before a test match while Richard addressed a luncheon gathering in the lounge upstairs. There were other similar examples.

I suppose the most famous of these was the 'car', as this cause célèbre has become known in New Zealand cricket history. The winner of the Cricketer of the Year award in Australia each year wins a flash car. The practice — generally, but not always — is for prizes to be pooled. So Man of the Match winnings and other prizemoney go into team funds, to be shared equally among all members of the side.

It's also reasonably common for the original recipient of a major prize to be treated a little more generously when funds are divvied up. The key to any policy is that it is always well and truly nutted out and accepted before any series begins. It's fair to say that in this ugly instance the terms and conditions were not understood or accepted by everyone in the team.

We hadn't won the overall award for Cricketer of the Year previously, so the car had never been a factor there. However, Hadlee had certainly won some major prizes before. In New Zealand in 1981–82, he won a Toyota car, the proceeds of which were split among all the team.

Not that we gave it a lot of thought, but I'm sure that while we were in Australia during the 1985–6 season, and were hammering the Aussies 2–1 in the test series, we all assumed any winnings would go into the team pool. A lot of our batsmen struck good form in the tests. Martin Crowe, John Reid, John Bracewell and Bruce Edgar all batted well at times. Hadlee towered over everyone, though, with his 33 wickets. In the Benson and Hedges one-day series that followed shortly after, Jeremy Coney, Martin Crowe, Richard himself, Bruce Edgar, Jeff Crowe and John Wright all had good innings, while Ewen Chatfield, Richard and Stu Gillespie shared the wickets pretty evenly.

We were eventually shaded by India for a place in the tournament final, but it was no surprise when Richard was chosen as the International Cricketer of the Year. What was a surprise was that he decided he wanted to keep the prize, an Alfa Romeo. A meeting was called in one of the lounges at Sydney airport and that's where Richard told us of his decision. He felt he'd played well, won the car in his own right and deserved to keep it.

This is typical of Richard in a way. He will look at something and then take a stand, even if it seems unreasonable or outrageous to others.

But the car announcement was a stunner. A vote was taken. The result was far from unanimous. This issue split our team, more than any other I can think of during my time in the side. The wrangle became public and bubbled on for quite some time.

Finally, it came to a head when we had a team meeting at Karori Park, Wellington, just before we were due to begin our home series against Australia in 1986.

It was a strange meeting because good mates were vigorously disagreeing with each other; John Wright, I remember, was happy for Richard to keep the car. Wrighty's opening partner, Bruce Edgar, normally a quiet, self-contained type, got extremely annoyed about the whole affair. Bruce believed totally in the team concept, pointed out that there was a precedent in this matter, and could see no possible justification for anyone setting himself apart from the team.

The talk went around and around. I was fairly ambivalent. I could see both sides, but really I just wanted the matter resolved peacefully, and, most importantly, I wanted Richard to play in the next game and to feel good about it so that he would

Richard Hadlee . . . liked being in the driver's seat.

be at his best. A compromise solution was worked out: Richard could keep the car if he made a contribution to team funds. The theory was that his contribution would be the Australian market value of the Alfa ($A14,000 back then), leaving him with a car worth double that on the New Zealand market.

Richard then mentioned that this would cause him tax problems and made a counter offer: one week's holiday for each player at a time-share resort in Taupo. The whole thing had gone on long enough and we were all keen to get back to beating the Aussies. I don't think any of us ever did spend any time in the time-share.

Eventually things settled down and Richard carried on taking packets of wickets, but it was an interesting insight into his thinking.

There were other times when he set himself apart. I've discussed elsewhere in this book the incident in our team dressing room before the Lancaster Park test against the West Indies in 1987, when he went quite close to withdrawing from the team.

Some players complained that Richard was selfish, that he was absorbed with setting records and with his own statistics. Richard would argue that statistics were a good motivational tool for him and that if they helped him play better and he took more wickets, well that must surely benefit the New Zealand team.

He was right, too. Put simply, I felt that we would win a test series if each of our players matched themselves against their equivalent in the opposition and that more of our players outperformed theirs. In those one-on-one confrontations Richard was seldom outplayed.

When you're a player, caught up in the tension of tests and tours, you can get quite worked up about some of these things. These days, as I look back, I'm more philosophical. In the end, you're there to win tests, not necessarily to make lifelong buddies. If you can all get on and enjoy each other's company on tour, so much the better, but your job is to play good cricket and support each other on the field.

Richard is a strange mixture. He can be very sensitive. I know he was extremely upset at the reaction when he decided to cut down the length of his run in the early 1980s. He was criticised by the public and the media and didn't feel he had the support of all his team. It really worried him, though it turned out to be a brilliant decision, one that prolonged his career by years.

A few years later, as he has related himself, he had something of a nervous breakdown and had to take a break in the Pacific Islands to try to put his life back in perspective. He worked closely with a Christchurch psychologist to get on top of his anxieties.

On the other hand, he likes to have a joke and is an extremely confident and capable public speaker. In fact, in most cricket countries in the world, he has made a pretty useful living out of speech-making.

It's not surprising that Richard divided opinion, even among his team-mates. If you believe in the tall-poppy theory, he was the tallest of tall poppies. I'm sure some of his team-mates felt envious of the media attention and financial rewards he got because of his cricket. They understood how good he was, but it would be only human nature for some not to be resentful.

I was always delighted to have Richard in any team I was in. If he played, he won us games and he also won us money. Richard retired at the end of the New Zealand season, in March 1990, and I worked hard to persuade him to make himself available for one last tour, to England a few months later.

He eventually relented. As usual he headed the test bowling averages and took the most wickets. There was a special honour for Richard just before the second test, at

Lord's, when he was knighted. He thus became the first player still active at test level to be knighted for his services to cricket.

As a selector, Richard has been more open and upfront than any of his predecessors. He is very happy to talk to the media, to explain his reasoning behind selections, and he has proved himself to be something of a gambler. He has been quick to introduce relatively inexperienced young players like Lou Vincent, Brendon McCullum, Ian Butler, Hamish Marshall, Kyle Mills, Brooke Walker, James Franklin, Paul Hitchcock and Jacob Oram to international cricket.

Outside of cricket Richard or Sir Richard, Paddles or Sir Paddles (or King Dick as Chris Kuggeleijn dubbed him) was a pretty conservative man. I can't recall seeing him at too many casino tables or having a punt on the nags, so it was testament to Kuggeleijn's negotiating skills that he was able to entice the champion bowler into a relatively large stake of a racehorse at one point.

There were some other noted careful spenders involved. The horse ran poorly and not too often either, putting paid to the theory that everything the great man touched turned to gold.

Richard's dress sense was a little like his bowling but only in the sense that it seldom strayed from the straight and narrow. He had a passion for grey trousers and black slip-on shoes. His team-mates on the 1986 tour of England decided to try to expand his fashion horizons by appointing him the dress marshall for the tour. He thus became the person whose task it was to set the dress standards for functions and team events.

We did this simply because we wanted him to see that in the wide world of clothing there were, in fact, some options. To our surprise and delight Richard arranged a deal for some free stuff from a manufacturer in England. Most cricketers are heavily into freebees so we turned up at the factory en masse and left armed with copious quantities of check shirts, dull trousers and v-neck jerseys. No one, Richard aside (and maybe Chatfield), had too much intention of wearing the stuff, but they did make great Christmas presents!

I remember batting with Richard at Eden Park against India in 1990 when we were deep in it. I joined him at wicket and asked for advice. He replied, 'If it's up, it's gonna go — good luck.' He smashed 83 in no time and we staged a pretty useful recovery.

Towards the end of the innings, he swept at a delivery from leg-spinner Narendra Hirwani and looked as if he had succeeded in getting a bottom edge. The ball sped to the boundary. To his dismay, the umpire at the time signalled leg-byes and that was that. Well, it would have been for most people. But Richard, after he was dismissed, went into the umpires' room at the tea break and demanded his extra four runs. Wouldn't you know it — he got them!

The official scoreboard reveals: Hadlee bowled Hirwani 87. Just like test wickets — test runs are test runs. A stats man to the end.

43. Nightmare at the Oval

The century Snedden didn't want

Martin Snedden, who these days is doing such a good job as Chief Executive of New Zealand Cricket, bowled himself into *Wisden* in the one-dayer against England at the Oval in 1983, but it's not a record he's proud of.

It was the first round of the 1983 World Cup. We'd had a good build-up, beating India and Australia and going through our warm-up games unbeaten. Martin was regarded as an important part of the attack, a dry medium-fast bowler who had shown an ability to bowl at the death.

At the Oval, the New Zealand attack comprised Hadlee, Lance Cairns, Snedden and Chatfield, with the fifth bowler's duties to be shared by Martin Crowe and Coney. England batted first and put in a solid effort. Chris Tavare made 45, David Gower 39, Mike Gatting 43, Ian Botham 22 and Graham Dilley 31 not out, but the innings was built around Allan Lamb, who scored at a run a ball in making a century.

Our bowling wasn't too bad, except for Martin, who was given a real pasting by Lamb. Hadlee did well — 12 overs for 26. Chatfield had 12 overs for 45 and Cairns, though a little expensive, got through his 12 overs for 57. Our captain, Geoff Howarth, had a bit of trouble with his fifth bowler. Jeremy Coney did well, bowling six overs for 20, but Martin Crowe was very expensive with six overs for 51.

Geoff obviously felt he had to bowl out Snedden, even if he was getting hit around. So Martin ended up with figures of 12 overs, 1 maiden, 105 runs, 2 wickets. He became the first bowler to concede 100 runs in a one-day international and still holds the record for the most runs conceded in such a match.

I doubt it was any consolation to him that by dismissing Lamb and Gatting, he

News Media Auckland

Martin Snedden . . . he made *Wisden*, but not how he'd have liked.

took more wickets than any other New Zealand bowler that day! By the end of the innings, he looked shell-shocked.

'I'd love to have come off,' he said years later, 'but Geoff obviously felt he didn't have another bowling option, so I had to bowl out. To make matters worse, it was a 60-over game, so I had to bowl 12 overs, rather than the usual 10.'

The nightmare bowling performance was not easily shrugged off. During the rest of the World Cup and then for the tour of England that followed, Martin was in and out of the top lineup. His confidence was affected by the hammering he took at the Oval.

He feels that it wasn't until he bowled so well against the West Indies at Christchurch in 1987 that he recovered his poise as a bowler. 'I lost all confidence after that effort against England. I would freeze up and struggle to bowl normally, and if I didn't make a reasonable start, I would be in trouble. I felt the guys were not that confident about my bowling.'

It's a tribute to Martin's determination that he eventually ended up being an 11-year veteran of international cricket. He would have played a lot more often had his career not coincided with a period when New Zealand pace-bowling resources were at their richest.

Through the 1980s, as Lance Cairns and then Ewen Chatfield retired, Martin became an indispensable part of the one-day team and played 93 one-day internationals. His 114 wickets placed him second to Richard Hadlee at the time of his retirement, and even now he is in the top half dozen or so. He also played 25 tests and took 58 wickets.

They're not figures he thought he'd ever achieve as he sat, stunned, in the dressing room at the Oval that evening in 1983.

These days of course he's the head man of New Zealand Cricket and an exceptionally good one at that. It's nice to know that when the Oval comes up in conversation, even the Boss is prepared to lose the odd battle!

44. In the spirit of good sportsmanship

The fine line between winning . . . and winning at all costs

The quest for wickets and runs is so intense at top level these days that sometimes sportsmanship disappears out the door. I'm all in favour of playing the game hard, but there must be a line that should not be crossed.

What is gamesmanship and what is cheating? There is a difference between a quick quip and persistent sledging, between a big appeal and charging an umpire, between expressing elation at gaining a wicket and giving a batsman a send-off.

New Zealanders have been involved in some unusual incidents down the years, some of which are inexplicable when considered under modern conditions.

In 1951, England opener Cyril Washbrook was given out lbw to New Zealand's inswing bowler Fen Cresswell's first delivery in a test at Christchurch. Washbrook was clearly annoyed at the decision and made his feelings known as he reluctantly departed, looking back over his shoulder unhappily. New Zealand captain Walter Hadlee, always a stickler for the spirit of cricket, asked Cresswell about the appeal and the decision. Cresswell said he regretted his appeal, saying he was now sure Washbrook had nicked the ball on to his pads. Hadlee then ran after Washbrook and recalled him to the wicket, withdrawing New Zealand's appeal.

Opinions were divided at the time. Some of the media gave Hadlee unstinting praise, others criticised him for undermining and embarrassing umpire Tonkinson. There was also criticism of Washbrook for not leaving the wicket immediately. Washbrook went on to make 58 in a drawn match.

I've spoken to Walter since about the incident and have no doubt he would do the same thing again, given the same circumstances. He would not have wanted to claim a wicket he did not believe had been taken fairly. While I applaud the spirit behind the Hadlee decision, I could not imagine a modern test captain being as generous. Cricketers these days adopt a swings and roundabouts philosophy — a fortunate decision you receive today is likely to be balanced by a bad one tomorrow.

There was less justification for the actions of New Zealand spin bowler Alec Moir the following season when New Zealand played the West Indies at Eden Park.

West Indies opener Allan Rae slipped when trying to regain his ground after being sent back by fellow opener Jeff Stollmeyer. The ball was returned to the bowler, Moir, who had an easy run-out opportunity, but chose not to remove the bails. At this point Rae was on 9. He went on to make 99.

Moir's actions have to be put in context. A few years earlier, Australian Lindsay Hassett refused to run out England's best batsman, Denis Compton, after Compton had dropped his bat in the middle of the pitch and stopped to get it. Fieldsmen would not be as generous as Moir and Hassett today. I see nothing wrong with running out a batsman who has slipped or dropped his bat and would equate it to a batsman continuing his innings after offering a chance and seeing the fieldsman drop it.

Ewen Chatfield's action in running out Derek Randall at Lancaster Park in 1978 was pushing things too far the other way. England was looking for quick runs in their second innings with a view to declaring — Ian Botham deliberately ran out his captain, Geoff Boycott, because he felt Boycott was batting too slowly. Randall, already like a greyhound between the wickets, was backing up aggressively and, in Chatfield's view, too early.

In such situations, with one team attempting to hit quick runs and the other defending for all its worth, tension mounts. Chats, normally a mild-mannered bloke, ran in, but did not deliver the ball. Instead he whipped off the bails and left Randall haring down the wicket to be run out by some distance. Mark Burgess, the New Zealand skipper, did his best to defend Chatfield, saying the non-striker should wait to see the ball in the air before leaving the crease. This is true, but still it is accepted that this sort of run out contravenes the spirit of cricket, if a formal warning has not been given first.

There were a few ticklish incidents during my career. Jeff Crowe recalled Allan Border at Adelaide in 1987 after Border had nicked one to him at slip. Jeff knew the ball hadn't carried and though Border was on his way to the pavilion, and his was the prized opposition wicket, Jeff called him back. It was a lucky day for Border. In the spirit of generosity, I had already missed stumping him off Evan Gray. It doesn't do to give these Aussies too many chances. Border went on to bat more than eight hours and made 205 in a big-scoring drawn match. If memory serves, Jeff won a French fair play award for his actions at Adelaide.

Jeff's sportsmanship was thrown into stark contrast in the next test, at Melbourne, when Andrew Jones, who was having a great tour, was given out caught

Greg Dyer . . . his test career ended after a catch he never took.

behind by wicketkeeper Greg Dyer, off Craig McDermott for 40. It seemed with the naked eye that Dyer had dropped the ball, and replays later confirmed that fact. However, Dyer appealed adamantly and Jones was given out. I believe that piece of cheating, which drew a lot of media attention, cost Dyer his international career. He was dropped from the Australian team shortly after and then Ian Healy established himself as the Aussie keeper.

In 1986, the Aussies accused me of cheating when I caught Greg Matthews in the Christchurch test. I knew I'd caught the ball fairly and the replays showed the ball had not bounced, but the Aussies were very unhappy. Border got quite sour on the whole thing and Matthews told me I would have to live with what I'd done for the rest of my life.

I've managed to do that fairly comfortably. Players are wise not to get too excited at times like these. Later in that tour, during the one-day series, there was an incident at Auckland from which Matthews himself didn't emerge too well. He caught Richard Hadlee right on the boundary's edge. Umpire Woodward initially signalled a six, but Matthews insisted he had caught the ball inside the field of play, so Hadlee walked. Replays later showed the umpire's original signal had been correct, for Matthews had caught the ball with one foot on the boundary rope.

The incident not only helped the Aussies draw the one-day series, but certainly cost Matthews a lot of popularity in New Zealand, as he discovered the next time he toured here.

45. All out for 26!

New Zealand's least fondly remembered scorecard

The most haunting number in New Zealand cricket? Surely it's 26. How does a test team get bowled out for 26? It happened to New Zealand at Eden Park in 1955. England, led by Len Hutton, and with famous bowlers like Frank Tyson, Brian Statham, Bob Appleyard and Johnny Wardle (all-rounder Trevor Bailey wasn't required), skittled New Zealand in their second innings for such an embarrassingly modest score that the section of *Wisden* reserved for lowest scores in test cricket is still headed by that effort.

I've often reflected on what that innings must have been like. Primary school teams I played in were often bowled out pretty quickly, but even we would have been a bit chastened to have made just 26. How must it have felt for the test side? Usually someone will go in and smash a few, or at least a couple of batsmen will nick some to the boundary and the score will get up to three figures.

When we played the West Indies at Christchurch in 1987, we needed just 33 for victory. In a way it was a no-win situation for our batsmen. There was no chance of playing a long innings, but there was every prospect of having to spend an uncomfortable hour or so struggling for runs while Malcolm Marshall, Anthony Gray, Joel Garner and Courtney Walsh unleashed a succession of thunderbolts at them.

Our batsmen struggled to apply themselves and we had quite a job to make even 33. At one point it was 13–3. Eventually Martin Crowe guided us to victory by five wickets, making 9 not out. The West Indies bowled just 10 overs and Marshall was not used, but Walsh and Gray were particularly hostile. It was not an impressive New Zealand batting performance but, even so, it was quite a bit better than 26 all out.

Heavens above — in 2001 Craig McMillan set a world test record by smacking 26 (4, 4, 4, 4, 6, 4) in one over, bowled by Younis Khan of Pakistan!

I've spoken to some of the New Zealanders who played in that infamous game

Don Neely Collection

The scoreboard from hell.

at Eden Park and they just shrug their shoulders. They seem to feel the events that day were so bizarre as to be inexplicable.

Tyson was the fastest bowler in the world, maybe the fastest of all time, and the other England bowlers were all top quality. But in the first innings, New Zealand had compiled 200 against the same attack. It wasn't the strongest of New Zealand batting lineups, but it did have in Bert Sutcliffe and John Reid two outstanding players and some others, like Geoff Rabone, who were capable of stubborn resistance.

The fall of wickets was amazing: 6, 8, 9, 14, 14, 22, 22, 22, 26, 26. Incredible though it seems, New Zealand began their second innings hoping they might win the test. They trailed by just 46 on the first innings and with England to bat last, thought they might put the visitors under pressure.

Instead, 105 minutes and 162 balls later, it was all over. Only Sutcliffe, 11, made double figures and only Harry Cave hit even one boundary. There weren't even any extras to bolster the New Zealand effort. Left-arm spinner Wardle bowled five overs and took 1–0. Off-cutter Appleyard was even more lethal: 4–7 off six overs.

It must have been pandemonium in the New Zealand dressing room. Players scrambling to get padded up, one defeated batsman after another returning disconsolate and the situation becoming ever grimmer.

There was a strange postscript to the match for me during the 2001–2 season. Tom Graveney, who opened the batting for England in that test, was leading a supporters' tour of New Zealand and when reminded of the Eden Park debacle, laughed and said: 'The really strange thing about it was that as we walked out to field for the second innings, Len Hutton looked at the scoreboard and said, "Just enough runs to win by an innings, eh." He was right.'

46. Players with the write stuff

Biographies now standard fare

Richard Hadlee was once asked whether he'd read a certain cricket book. 'I don't read cricket books; I write 'em,' said Richard with a sparkle in his eye. He's right, too. Richard has written and co-written all sorts of books: biographical, coaching and humorous.

Cricketers generally aren't great cricket readers, which is a little odd considering the vast number of books there are about the game. Among my team-mates, Martin Crowe and Martin Snedden, who both came from cricket families with long involvement in the game, had read widely about cricket's history and were as comfortable discussing Jack Hobbs and Wally Hammond as they were Viv Richards and Allan Border. Others had read very little.

I fall about in the middle. I used to eagerly await the arrival each year of the *Cricket Almanack* and I would devour the *DB Cricket Annual*, compiled for so long by Don Neely. But I've never been a great reader of cricket history. I did set out to read Dick Brittenden's *Silver Fern on the Veldt*, the story of New Zealand's famous 1953–54 tour of South Africa, but I'm not absolutely sure I finished it.

As I got older I did enjoy the writing of certain journalists, Brittenden, of the *Christchurch Press*, and Don Cameron, of the *New Zealand Herald*, in particular.

Then I went through another stage. After I'd been in the New Zealand team for a few years, some of my team-mates and former team-mates began to have their books published. I'd already read *My Way*, by Glenn Turner, an interesting read at the time. Lance Cairns, riding the crest of his popularity after his spectacular hitting in Australia, produced *Give It A Heave*, which was a generally light read. I don't know

Actually Ken, it was a hell of a good way to make a living.

what Lance thinks of his book now, but I'd suggest that, judging by some of his strongly opinionated column writing in the *Sunday News* over the past few years, he'd call his book *Give It A Serve* if he wrote it now.

Two books I very much enjoyed were the autobiographies of Jeremy Coney and John Wright. Even though I'd played for years with both of them, I found their books informative and humorous. Even the titles, *The Playing Mantis* and *Christmas in Rarotonga*, were off-beat.

There have been so many books over the past decade that it has been harder to keep up. Sometimes I wonder if players ever regret some of the things they put in their books, perhaps to get a headline and sell another hundred copies.

Ken Rutherford wrote a book called *A Hell of a Way to Make a Living*. I thought Ken let himself down a little by being too cynical about his former team-mates. Playing cricket isn't a bad way to make a living, when all's said and done. Sometimes I look forward to a book and feel the player hasn't done himself justice. Geoff Howarth was a super batsman at his best and a really fine skipper, but his biography didn't truly reflect his standing. He had more to say than what was in his book.

I'm a strong admirer of Richie Benaud. I enjoy working with him in the commentary box and find he is full of common sense. Therefore I made sure I read his autobiography, *Willow Patterns*, as soon as I could get my hands on it. I wasn't disappointed.

One of the more recent New Zealand books I've looked through is Adam Parore's *The Wicked-Keeper*. Adam's book was an interesting concept, as it included a lot of comment from other players. I thought Adam portrayed himself fairly honestly in his book and left it for others to judge him.

I guess the book I'm waiting for is John Bracewell's. Braces is still heavily involved in cricket, coaching Gloucestershire. No doubt he has hopes of coaching internationally after that. So perhaps we may have to wait a while yet for his book, but I have a feeling it'll be worth the wait. Knowing Braces, his book should be a ripper!

47. Players who knew no boundaries

Cricketers who excelled in other sports arenas

New Zealand's best cricketers have often excelled at other sports. There have been seven double All Blacks, the term given to men who have represented New Zealand at both international cricket and rugby. This elite group is: George Dickinson, Charlie Oliver, Curly Page, Eric Tindill, Bill Carson, Brian McKechnie and Jeff Wilson. Of the seven, only Tindill played at test level in both codes. McKechnie and Wilson played at one-day international cricket for New Zealand, but missed test selection.

Cricketers have excelled in many sports besides rugby. Verdun Scott, the opening batsman in the immediate Second World War years, was a fine rugby league player, who travelled to Britain with the 1939 Kiwis. It was Scott's misfortune that the tour was abandoned after just two matches because of the outbreak of war. With the two round-the-world boat journeys, it was a long time away for not much sport.

Leonard Cuff, a national long jump champion, and the founder of the Olympic movement in this country, captained the 1897 New Zealand cricket team that played Queensland. Phil Horne, our opening batsman during the 1980s, was a New Zealand badminton representative.

One unusual example was Ken Hough, who toured New Zealand with the 1948 Australian soccer team, then moved to this country a few years later. He represented New Zealand in six tests, as a fast bowler, before returning to Australia. Hough, though good enough to play test cricket for New Zealand, never did make the New South Wales side. The Hough example reminds me of batting maestro Martin Donnelly, who averaged more than 50 in tests for New Zealand and played in one rugby test — for England.

The multi-talented Eric Tindill, as depicted by the Wellington Sports Post.

Left-arm bowler Arthur Fisher not only played for New Zealand from 1895 to 1907, but also was the New Zealand amateur golf champion in 1904 and a hugely successful race horse owner.

Soccer has given New Zealand several double internationals. The first two were Edmund Vernon Sale and Ces Dacre, the punishing batsman of the 1920s. Then came Don McRae and Hough. In the 1960s and early 1970s, cricketers Grahame Bilby, Vic Pollard and Mark Burgess all played soccer for New Zealand.

Left-arm spinner Tom Burtt played hockey for New Zealand before the war and cricket for New Zealand after it. Gordon Rowe represented New Zealand at both sports at much the same time, and two decades later Keith Thomson did so as well.

Besides those who have reached test level, a number of other famous sportsmen went close to reaching top level in two sports. Anthony Wilding, New Zealand's only Wimbledon tennis champion, represented Canterbury at the turn of the 20th century and in one match in 1901, against Auckland, scored 28 and took 3–35. His father, Frank, played cricket for New Zealand. My first junior representative cricket captain was Clive Currie, who went on to play for Wellington and represent the All Blacks. Clive had the ability to go even further than he did in cricket.

Peter Petherick, the Otago off-spinner of the 1970s, took up lawn bowls seriously on closing his cricket career and went within a whisker of representing New Zealand at that sport, too. Two famous All Blacks, Ron Hemi and Don Clarke, played Plunket Shield cricket through the 1950s. Clarke, a pace bowler, all but made the 1958 New Zealand cricket team to England and was one of the Northern Districts bowlers the day John Reid hit 15 sixes in an innings at the Basin in 1963.

The case of Jeff Wilson is a reminder of how much more difficult it is these days for players to compete at the top level in two sports. Several dozen New Zealand cricket representatives also played provincial rugby. But with cricket now played all year and rugby having gone professional, the chances of that happening have decreased dramatically. Wilson certainly had the talent to play test cricket, but except for a series of one-dayers against Australia in 1993, he was largely lost to cricket while he was an All Black. It was only after retiring from rugby in 2002 that he was able to turn his attention again to cricket.

48. Hidden terror
on the tarmac

Running eights on the world's fastest outfield

In the 1940s, Sir Carl Berendsen was New Zealand's Ambassador to the United States and our Permanent Representative at the United Nations.

Long before that, in his early days as a civil servant, he was the Wellington representative wicketkeeper. In his unpublished autobiography, he told of a club match in which he hit an eight.

'I mean an eight,' he wrote. 'I got the ball away to fine leg for three, the return was overthrown and we ran three more, when it was again thrown wildly we ran another two. Eight for one stroke seemed pretty good to me, but I was greatly deflated the next day when the newspaper reported that Berendsen had hit the only eight of the day. Of the day, be it noted; of the century, I felt!'

For a couple of months in 1949, Tom Larkin worked under Sir Carl at the United Nations. Tom has been one of the enduring and popular figures in Wellington cricket. He was introduced to top cricket early, for his best mate at school in New Plymouth was the incomparable Martin Donnelly and they remained lifelong friends.

'Had I known about Sir Carl's eight,' said Tom, 'I could have given him a new perspective, for I once played in a match in which an eight was not exceptional.

'In 1944, I was put in command of a harbour defence motor launch, with the responsibility of local patrol of the coastline near Beirut, in Lebanon. By that time, the war had shifted to the western Mediterranean, along the North African coast, and to Italy. For us, the biggest danger was boredom.

'To offset this, I managed to borrow some cricket gear and arranged some matches against service and other teams located in and near Beirut. Our motor launch had a crew of 12, including me, so for each game I would leave one sailor on watch and lead the remaining 11 to play. We were the oddest possible group, England, Scots and Irish, and only half of them had any experience of cricket. But they were all keen to play, if only as a diversion.

'The game I remember best was played against an air force team stationed not far from the city. To our astonishment, the playing surface was the airfield itself. It seemed to stretch endlessly into the distance on every side and in the centre was the pitch, marked out in the regulation manner, but with the stumps at each end lodged carefully in tailored blocks of wood.

'We were told that because the surface was so hard, the ball when hit would travel far and fast. Accordingly, the playing surface was extended to something like twice the normal size. "But," we were told reassuringly, "boundaries count only four." Little did we reckon on what that implied.

'I remember that we bowled first and that setting the field in the usual positions or at the usual distances was useless, since the ball, when hit, raced rapidly past all but the most nimble fieldsmen and sped away in the far distance.

'At first, a single fieldsmen would give chase, but since few of our team could throw very well, relays of helpers became necessary. Balls that did not reach the boundary were returned in laborious steps to the bowler or the wicketkeeper through several pairs of hands. Meanwhile the batsmen were running and running and running. Six, seven, eight and even nine runs were possible from a simple shot, until we decided that the easiest way to keep down the score was simply to let the ball cross the boundary for four.

'I don't remember what the scores were. Had the air force team been very good (and I don't recall that they were) they could have scored about a thousand. All I remember is that by the time we batted we were exhausted and hardly able to exploit the advantages that the vast ground afforded.

'Had there been a newspaper report, however, there would have been no reference to "the only eight of the day". There were many more than that.'

49. They can duck, but they can't hide

Notable noughts in test cricket

Every cricketer will have a story about making a duck. Unfortunately, New Zealanders have made more than their share in test cricket.

Glenn Turner opened his test career with a duck — caught Sobers, bowled Hall at Eden Park in 1969. Fortunately for Turner, this was not a case of beginning as he meant to go on. Turner didn't play his last test for another 14 years and in that time never recorded another test duck.

The first test between England and New Zealand in July 1983 at the Oval provided ducks with a difference. The match was a family honour for the Crowes of Auckland, for Jeff and Martin appeared in a test match together for the first time, making them at that time only the fourth set of brothers to have achieved that honour for New Zealand (the Hadlees, Howarths and Parkers preceded them). In the first innings, Jeff and Martin were both dismissed without scoring. The English tabloids had a field day as the umpire who gave them out was Dickie Bird — so we had both Crowes making ducks courtesy of Bird.

Only one New Zealander has made the ultimate test duck — out first ball in a test. That was John Morrison, who was caught Mike Hendrick, bowled Geoff Arnold against England at Christchurch in 1975. John Wright escaped a similar fate by a whisker at the Basin Reserve three years later, when he edged the first ball Bob Willis delivered to wicketkeeper Bob Taylor, only to see umpire Bob Monteith turn down the appeal. The gale force wind at the Basin made umpiring difficult that day and helped Wright escape.

Danny Morrison was something of a duck expert. In the list of batsmen who have

Danny Morrison, the batsman. What happened to the bails, Danny?

made most test ducks, Danny is outstanding. The list is topped by West Indian Courtney Walsh, who made 43 ducks in 185 innings. But Danny's effort of 24 ducks from 71 innings is statistically much more (or less) impressive.

At the time of writing, leading duck scorers in test cricket are:

Ducks		Innings
43	Courtney Walsh (West Indies)	185
27	Shane Warne (Australia)	142
26	Curtly Ambrose (West Indies)	145
25	Glenn McGrath (Australia)	99
24	Danny Morrison (New Zealand)	71

Danny's fifth placing is quite extraordinary, especially when it is considered he wasn't a bunny as a batsman. He had a top score of 42 in a test and at Eden Park in 1997 he and Nathan Astle saved the test against England when they had an unbroken partnership of 106 for the last wicket. Danny made 14 not out that day, and stuck around for 165 minutes, facing 133 balls, to not only enable Astle to reach his century, but to save the test.

Besides Danny, other New Zealanders with at least 10 test ducks have been Ken Rutherford (16 from 99 innings), John Bracewell (13 from 60), Bob Blair (12 from 34, a remarkable ratio), Dick Motz (12 from 56), Richard Hadlee (12 from 134), Ewen Chatfield (11 from 54, a figure which would have been higher but for Chats' 33 not outs in tests), Daniel Vettori (11 from 62), Stephen Boock (10 from 41), Dipak Patel (10 from 66) and Simon Doull (10 from 50).

> **Danny once scored four consecutive test ducks, in 1993–94, repeating the feat of Murphy Su'a the previous season and Lawrie Miller in 1953–54. Miller's horror run was more remarkable because he was a batsman.**

For all Danny's duck-scoring feats, Chris Martin and Geoff Allott are really the kings as far as I'm concerned. Between 2000 and 2002, Martin had eight consecutive innings in which he failed to score, including the odd 0 not out. This outstrips previous bests by New Zealanders. Both Johnny Hayes and Michael Owens had five consecutive scoreless innings, including not outs, in tests.

Allott held a test record of sorts for a time, failing to score in more than half his test innings. He improved this figure slightly towards the end of his career and eventually played 15 test innings, failing to score in six of them. He also holds the world record for batting the longest time in a test without getting off the mark. In March 1999, Allott batted 101 minutes against South Africa at Eden Park without bothering the scorers. This beat by four minutes the record set by Godfrey Evans, the England wicketkeeper, against Australia at Adelaide in 1947.

Allott and Chris Harris fought defiantly to prevent South Africa pressing for victory. After South Africa had totalled a massive 621–5 declared, New Zealand struggled to 320–9. In came Allott. He and Harris survived the next 27 overs — 101 minutes — in adding 32 runs. This soaked up valuable time and New Zealand, following on, were able to hold on for a draw. As Evans had, Allott several times declined opportunities to score before eventually being dismissed caught Pollock, bowled Kallis for one of the more eventful ducks. In a nice touch, the scorers presented him with a copy of a run chart of his innings.

In the spirit of bowlers fighting to help their side, I should mention Martin Snedden's effort against Australia at the Basin Reserve in 1990. Martin was promoted to nightwatchman on the second day of the match and was 0 not out overnight. The following day he was at his most obdurate and did not score for over after over. Even when he finally got under way, he picked up runs at only a trickle, eventually scoring 23 in just under three hours. His gutsy effort did, however, help put New Zealand in a position to win the test.

Even worse than a duck, I suppose, is making a pair — two ducks in one match. Two New Zealand captains have suffered this ignominy, Harry Cave against the West Indies in 1956 and Stephen Fleming against Australia at Hobart in 1997.

Too many New Zealanders have made a pair on test debut. The three most recent have been Ken Rutherford, against the West Indies in Port of Spain in 1985, Chris Kuggeleijn against India at Bangalore in 1988 and James Franklin against Pakistan at Auckland in 2001. At least Kuggeleijn achieved one notable feat in that match at Bangalore. It was Kuggs who caught Arun Lal to give Richard Hadlee his world record 382nd test wicket.

There's no doubt that there has always been a fascination about ducks in cricket. I suppose it's because cricket is such a statistically orientated game, but it is remarkable that so many players have received such vast amounts of coverage down the years for batting so unsuccessfully!

Footnote: I should mention Richard Hadlee in this item on ducks. It's not that he scored particularly many, but he sure caused a few. In fact, Richard dismissed 66 batsmen for ducks in test cricket, the world record.

50. Treading the Basin boards

Scoreboard 'home' for some famous names

For years, any young lad in Wellington who was keen on cricket seemed to do a stint on the Basin Reserve scoreboard. It was a tradition that went on for decades.

Veteran broadcaster Peter Sellers was a sports-mad teenager when he worked the scoreboard during New Zealand's last game before the Second World War, against Sir Julian Cahn's team in 1939.

Through the early 1950s, a youngster from Wellington College named Ron Brierley worked on the scoreboard and, I'm told, turned it into quite a profitable business. He would deal with the Wellington association, taking payment for himself and a couple of other boys he was to employ. Sometimes he would 'forget' to employ the full complement, working harder himself, but also making double pay. A budding entrepreneur.

I worked on the scoreboard during the late 1960s and early 1970s, when people like Bruce Murray, Grahame Bilby, Barry Sinclair, Ian Therkleson, Mike Coles and Richard Collinge were playing for Wellington. While on the scoreboard I had my first look at Murray Webb's pace side on when he played for Otago against Wellington. He looked terrifying, especially with that enormous leap before he delivered the ball.

The scoreboard, on the eastern side of the Basin, was always something of a danger. It had a ladder that had to be climbed vertically and in the high winds it used to wobble about. Of more concern were the large square metal plates on which numbers and letters were printed. They were fixed in place, somewhat precariously, by hooking them over a nail protruding from the board. When it got windy, which was not uncommon at the Basin, the plates would fly off the

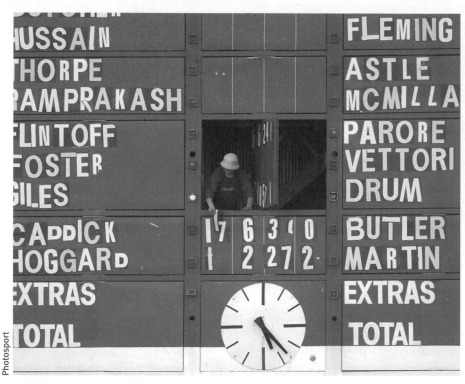

The Basin Reserve scoreboard — 'It looks like a ransom note.'

scoreboard and threaten everyone nearby with decapitation.

Despite the problems, it was great fun on that scoreboard. We boys would get to know the scorers in the box next door very well. I felt right at home. The chief scorer was Ian Smith of the Kilbirnie club, the club I supported. The main radio commentator at that time was Trevor Rigby, another stalwart of the Kilbirnie club and a very keen soccer man as well, which increased his stature still further in my eyes, for I played soccer, too.

I suppose a big attraction when operating any scoreboard is that it takes you closer to the game itself. It enables you to dream. I'd imagine myself actually being out there in the middle, playing on the Basin.

My first and only opportunity to play at the old Basin came in 1973 for Stewie Dempster's 'All Stars' team against Canterbury. I can well remember the long walk from the old deck chairs out to the middle. It wasn't a long innings — a first ball duck, bowled playing across the line! Mr Dempster's team included some interesting names, including future test players Bruce Edgar, Evan Gray and Robert Vance, future All Black Clive Currie and spin bowler Graeme Steel, who these days runs the New Zealand Sports Drug Agency.

Mr Dempster and his fellow selectors, having seen what I had to offer, sent me back to pasture confident that I needed more time. Seven years elapsed, with more time spent in the nets than on the scoreboard, before I Smith returned to the now remodelled Basin for a debut home test against India, and a more profitable match than my previous one on the ground.

The big scoreboard was a fixture at the Basin for half a century until the Basin was remodelled in 1978–80. It was replaced by a flash semi-automatic scoreboard situated at the southern end of the ground.

This scoreboard has generally been informative and efficient, though I miss seeing boys scampering up and down altering it.

The new scoreboard was back in the news again at the end of the 2002 season when it fell into amazing disrepair. There was trouble with the electronics; some days it was working and other days it wasn't.

Even more bizarre, there seemed to be all sorts of problems with the lettering. Gone were the standard letters we spectators were used to. In their place was the strangest hotch-potch of letters, some turned upside down, you'd ever see. Jeremy Coney, with that priceless wit of his, was spot on when he described the scoreboard as looking like a ransom note.

51. Humbled by the Aussies after years of waiting

New Zealand's first test against Australia

It took New Zealand many years of trying before Australia would deign to play us in a test. There were a few tours by Australian selections, and sometimes an Australian team would stop off in New Zealand on the way to England for an Ashes series. But pinning them down to a test series was nearly impossible.

Finally, immediately after the Second World War, the Aussies agreed. They would come over to New Zealand in early 1946 and play a few matches, including one test. (It was only some years later that the test was accorded official status.)

From New Zealand's point of view, the timing couldn't have been worse. Our two greatest batsmen of the time, Martin Donnelly and Bert Sutcliffe, were overseas after extended war duty. Australia, on the other hand, fielded a team of legends. True, Don Bradman was missing, as he was ill. But look at this cricket who's who: Bill Brown, Ken Meuleman, Sid Barnes, Keith Miller, Lindsay Hassett, Colin McCool, Ian Johnson, Don Tallon, Ray Lindwall, Ernie Toshack, Bill O'Reilly! Five of them would be serious candidates for an all-time Australian team and most of them were or became leading world cricketers.

Against them, New Zealand fielded perhaps their weakest test team ever. Mac Anderson, Ces Burke, Len Butterfield, Don McRae, Charles Rowe and Verdun Scott were making their test debuts, and pace bowler Don Cleverley was playing his first test since 1932!

I've spoken to Walter Hadlee, the New Zealand captain, about this match and there's no doubt it grated a little with him. The game was played at the Basin Reserve at the end of March 1946. There had been a lot of rain in Wellington in the lead-up,

Not the greatest test in New Zealand cricket history.

but the first day of scheduled play dawned bright and sunny. 'Bill Brown, who was the Australian captain, and I went out to inspect the wicket,' Walter told me. 'It was unplayable. But we looked around and there was a huge crowd in. There'd been a long war and people were hungry to see international cricket again.

'Bill and I talked it over and we had a new pitch cut beside the prepared one, which was far too muddy to be used. I won the toss, which I didn't want to do, and eventually decided to bat. It was cloudy and as the outfield was wet, I thought it might inconvenience the Australian bowlers.

'Instead, no sooner had I elected to bat than the sun came out. It turned the wicket into a real sticky and the Australian bowlers had a field day. Toshack, left-arm medium-pace, and O'Reilly, medium-pace leg-spin and googlies, were nearly unplayable.'

The New Zealand innings turned into a procession. Only Verdun Scott (14) and Merv Wallace (10) made more than six. New Zealand were bowled out for 42, the last eight wickets falling for five runs. O'Reilly had 5–14 and Toshack 4–12. It was embarrassing.

In reply, the Australians struggled against the fine pace bowling of Jack Cowie, who took 6–40. Eventually the visitors got to 199–8. Brown declared on the second morning when it became clear how spiteful the pitch had become. Hadlee felt if Australia had had to bat against their own bowling, they might not have fared much better than the New Zealanders had.

The New Zealand second innings was as quick as the first. This time only Wallace (14) and wicketkeeper Eric Tindill (13) reached double figures. New Zealand was dismissed for 54. In the two New Zealand innings, there were six ducks and Rowe and Butterfield recorded pairs. Anderson, Butterfield, McRae, Rowe and Cleverley never played for New Zealand again. New Zealand batted only 71 overs in total in this match.

So Australia, despite making fewer than 200, won by an innings and 103 runs.

The debacle had lasting effects. For decades Australia declined to play New Zealand in a test and was always able to refer to the game at the Basin. Instead they sent over a succession of 'B' teams, using New Zealand conditions to prepare their players for tours of England, but never offering to put their apparent superiority on the line.

The Aussies finally relented in 1973–4 when home and away series were played. Is it any wonder there was such rejoicing when New Zealand won the test at Lancaster Park that season?

52. 'Bula' was always close enough

Tongue-twisters from the commentary position

Up in the television commentary box, we are at pains to try to pronounce players' names correctly. It's a sign of sloppy work when a broadcaster can't get a name right. Some of the Sri Lankans, in particular, have presented a challenge over the years. When they arrived in New Zealand for their first tour of our country, in 1983, names such as Ranjan Madugalle, Sidath and Mithra Wettimuny, Rumesh Ratnayake and Yohan Goonasekera were all new to cricket followers.

Over the years, the Sri Lankans have offered us such tongue-twisters as Tillakaratne, Ranatunga, Gurusinha, Muralitharan, Dunusinghe, Wickramasinghe, Pushpakumara, Ramanayake, Samarasekera, Jayasuriya, Wijegunawardene, Kaluwitharana, Jayawardene, Dharmasena, Upashantha, Weeraratne, Sangakkara, Gunawardene, Jayasekera, Hathurusinghe, Madurasinghe, Warnaweera and Senanayaka. And they're just the surnames. Sometimes, even when you get a surname that's manageable, the first names can be something of an obstacle. For instance, Ellawalakankanamge Asoka Ranjith de Silva and Pinnaduwage Aravinda de Silva.

Off-spinner Muttiah Muralitharan has caused more problems than most. The continuing poser is whether his surname should be pronounced Murali-daran or Mura-litharan — 'th' or 'd'? To the best of my knowledge, this has never been resolved. Even the Sri Lankans themselves seem unsure.

One day when our television crew was in Christchurch, Sir Howard Morrison rang us at Lancaster Park to help us in our pronunciation of Parore. He advised us that it was Paror-ay. We passed the phone around so that everyone got the message. Shortly after, we went and asked the man himself, and Adam told us to continue

That's Bula, back row, third from left. He looks like just another cricketer, but what a surname!

pronouncing his surname as we had always done. That was good enough for us. Sir Howard was at that time also mounting a one-man campaign to have All Black loose forward Taine Randell's first name pronounced Tay-ee-nay. He may well have been correct, but again we've tended to go with the way everyone in New Zealand says it, including the player himself.

There have been other teasers in international cricket. Venkat of India is regarded as one of the world's best umpires today. Back in 1965, when John Reid's New Zealand ran into him, he was a world-class spinner. His full name is Srinivas Venkataraghavan, and the New Zealanders nicknamed him Rent-A-Caravan.

All this is mere preamble, though, to mention of the international cricketer who toured New Zealand three times from 1948 to 1962 and presented the biggest possible challenge to journalists, broadcasters and scoreboard attendants. The man in question was a big-hitting Fijian cricketer who was invariably called Bula. He delighted crowds everywhere with his massive six-hitting and his sunny personality. He'd have caused more furrowed eyebrows if he'd insisted on being addressed by his full surname — Bulamainavaleniveivakabulaimainavolakebalao. His surname was derived from the story of how the joyous news of his birth was the key to his grandfather's rapid recovery from a serious illness.

I'm glad I never had to cope with that one while broadcasting live on television. Somehow Ian Smith pales by comparison!

53. One that got away

How Clarrie Grimmett was lost to Australia

Until the arrival of Richard Hadlee, New Zealand hadn't produced many genuinely champion bowlers. Perhaps Jack Cowie would have been, but for the fact that he lost his best years to the Second World War.

It makes the case of Clarrie Grimmett all the sadder. Grimmett was the first great New Zealand bowler. Unfortunately, he had to go to Australia to prove himself.

As Grimmett's leg-spin developed, just before the First World War, he found that New Zealand cricket, still in its international infancy, did not give him the opportunities he wanted, so he moved to Australia.

From the time he arrived in Australia, the Grimmett story is well enough known. He lived up to that famous expression, 'If at first you don't succeed try and try again.' Grimmett, known variously as Grum, Scarlet and The Gnome, did not break into Sheffield Shield cricket until he was 32 and made his test debut at 34 — many bowlers are long retired by then — yet in 37 tests took a world record 216 scalps. He took the most wickets in first-class cricket, 1424, by a bowler who did not play county cricket.

It's interesting to note that one Richie Benaud, a fair judge one would have thought, has Grimmett either in or very close to his World XI of all time.

Grimmett was born at Caversham, Dunedin, on Christmas Day 1891. His family moved to Wellington soon after, and he attended Mount Cook School, where he fancied himself as a fast bowler. A school sports master realised he had the physique and temperament of a spinner and a successful transition was made.

He made his first-class debut for Wellington against Auckland in 1912, taking 4–48 in the second innings. Over the next couple of seasons, he had two five-wicket hauls and, opening the batting, scored usefully. In 1914 he played two matches against Arthur Sims' Australian side and another against Dan Reese's Canterbury XI. But he was extremely disappointed to miss selection for Reese's New Zealand team to

Clarrie Grimmett . . . New Zealand's gift to Australian cricket.

Australia in 1913–14, being named a reserve.

He decided to chance his arm across the Tasman, and after stints at Sydney and Melbourne finally found recognition when he moved to Adelaide. When he was 44 years of age, he took 44 wickets in a series in South Africa, but he was controversially overlooked for Australian teams after that.

Grimmett returned to New Zealand for one tour, in 1927–28, by which time he was a star in the Australian side. In six first-class matches, he took 47 wickets at under 17 each. He took 7–159 in the Wellington match, 12–151 against Otago, 7–115 against Canterbury, 9–171 against Auckland, 3–100 and 9–99 against New Zealand.

His success on this tour led to a curious letter to him from Dan Reese, who had become the president of the New Zealand Cricket Council. The letter reads:

My Dear Grimmett

I have just read your letter to my brother [historian Tom Reese], giving him some of the particulars he wanted in connection with your cricket career. I note that you express your wish for an opportunity of re-visiting New Zealand so as to be able to renew your old acquaintances here.

Apart from the pleasure it would give you, I am sure you would be a great attraction for the cricketing public on this side and so I have just dropped a private note to Hugh Trumble asking if he can include you in the Australian Eleven which is due to come to New Zealand in February and March. As Vic Richardson is one of the Selectors, you might take the opportunity of notifying him that you are available and would like to come.

I have always been sorry that I did not see more of you before we picked that New Zealand team for Australia in 1913. Of course we had seen very little of you at that time, but I always remember that Harry Trott spoke well of your ability. It would not have hurt to have both you and Sandman in the side. However, that is all done with now.

New Zealand is very proud of your progress in the game and your eventually gaining International honours. It is the first time a New Zealand Cricketer has ever appeared in this class of cricket.

Kind regards
Yours sincerely
Daniel Reese

PS: You will understand that my letter has been written privately to Trumble for the Australians would not stand us dictating as to who are to come over here in the Australian team, so please treat this matter confidentially as far as you are concerned.

Under completely different circumstances, in the early 1990s New Zealand lost the services of former Cantabrian Andy Caddick to England. Caddick is one of the world's best seamers and has done some fine work for the England test team. Before he had broken into the England team, Martin Crowe rang him and offered him the chance to play test cricket for New Zealand, but Caddick by then had his sights set on representing England, and that was that.

Fortunately, we have managed to retain most of our talent, the latest example of a player returning home to represent New Zealand being Lou Vincent.

54. Girls on top of the world

White Ferns win the World Cup

Twenty-three December 2000 is by far the most significant date in New Zealand women's cricket history. It was on that day that New Zealand won the women's World Cup, beating long-time rivals Australia in a truly gripping and high-quality final at the Brierley Oval in Christchurch.

I was part of a full television commentary team that covered the game live and must say I had my fingers crossed beforehand. We'd covered the New Zealand-India semi-final three days earlier and that was a mediocre match. India was bowled out for 117 in 45 overs and New Zealand passed that total in just 26 overs. The game was not a great advertisement for women's cricket, which was a pity because this was by far the best opportunity the women's game had ever had to advance its cause in New Zealand.

The other semi-final was marginally better. South Africa reached 180–8 in their 50 overs, but Australia passed that total in just 31 overs. Australian openers Belinda Clark and Lisa Keightley put on 170 for the first wicket and that was that.

Though the New Zealand women's team — the White Ferns — have had some good wins down the years, it would be fair to say that Australia have generally had the better of them. The situation in women's cricket is not dissimilar to that in netball, where two or three teams dominate the world stage.

I felt that on tournament form, Australia would go into the final favoured to win. They had some outstanding top-order batting and in Cathryn Fitzpatrick the fastest bowler in the tournament. However, it was noticeable what an efficient and competent all-round unit New Zealand had become.

Photosport

The greatest moment in New Zealand women's cricket . . . Clare Nicholson has Charmaine Mason caught behind by Rebecca Rolls and the White Ferns are world champions.

Credit for this must be given to their coach Mike Shrimpton, who has always been very strong on the technical side of the game. His influence was clear.

New Zealand batted first in the final and fought doggedly to get to 184. Disappointingly, they were bowled out in the 48th over, which is poor cricket in a one-day international. A number of the batters got starts but the highest score was Kathryn Ramel's 41. In the context of the game, this was a match-winning innings. She scored it off just 63 balls. Earlier Rebecca Rolls (34), Emily Drumm (21) and Debbie Hockley (24) had battled hard, without ever looking to be in charge. Most of the batters hung around long enough to contribute at least a few

World champion smiles form the 2000 New Zealand women's team.

runs and in the end this proved very important.

As Australian openers Keightley and Clark walked out to begin their team's innings, the odds favoured Australia, though locals felt that 184 was at least a competitive total.

The key moment of the Australian innings was the dismissal of captain Clark for 91, scored from just 102 balls. She was placing the ball so well, and running so hard between the wickets, that if she'd remained at the wicket she would certainly have guided her team to victory. When Clark was bowled by Clare Nicholson, the complexion of the match changed.

The New Zealanders bowled well. Katrina Keenan, Rachel Pullar and Nicholson all claimed two wickets, but I thought Catherine Campbell's spell of 10 overs, 1–28 was critical late in the Australian innings. The fielding of Helen Watson was decisive. She was responsible for two run outs including, in the first over, the form batsman of the tournament, Keightley.

For most of the day it was obvious the game was going to turn out to be a thriller.

There was certainly plenty of drama, none more so than when Fitzpatrick was given out bowled (by Ramel). This required a third umpire decision, it eventually being adjudged that the ball had brushed the leg stump on the way through.

It got to the stage where Australia required 10 runs off 11 balls, and then, at the start of the last over, five runs. But they were nine wickets down. With her first delivery, not a great one, Nicholson had Charmaine Mason caught behind by Rolls — from a wicketkeeper's perspective I know what a sweet feeling it must have been for Rolls when the ball stuck in those gloves — and there was the sight of Nicholson charging towards her wicketkeeper to celebrate.

New Zealand had won by four runs with five balls remaining.

The game was a challenge to commentate, even though it fluctuated all day and was always close. We commentators had statistician extraordinaire Francis Payne feeding us all sorts of facts and figures, but none of us had the background knowledge of women's cricket that we did of the men's game. It was a little like doing NPC first division rugby all season, then switching across to do the third-division semi-final. The game is the same, but the players are all new.

People have often asked me how I compare women's and men's cricket. To be honest, I try not to. It's like asking how Serena Williams would go against Lleyton Hewitt. Obviously Williams would probably not win a single game, but that does not mean her brand of tennis is not good.

In women's cricket, the batters especially are generally good. The top batters — players like Belinda Clark and New Zealand's Emily Drumm — are fine players. They play a wide array of shots and do things like running between the wickets really well. It seems they hit harder than some of their team-mates, but that's because they time the ball well.

Having said that, they are not facing great bowling. The pace of the women's version of cricket is much slower. Batters are not put under nearly the same pressure.

In retrospect, that World Cup win in Christchurch was the culmination of a decade of behind-the-scenes work, and not just the standard of cricket played by stars like Hockley, Drumm, Rolls, Keenan and the rest of them, and the coaching of Shrimpton. It was also a reflection of the increasingly professional way the game has been administered since it amalgamated with men's cricket and all came under the umbrella of New Zealand Cricket.

It should not be overlooked that this was the first time New Zealand had won a cricket World Cup, men or women. The result earned New Zealand women's cricket a huge amount of credibility.

The flow-down effects of that exciting win in Christchurch were obvious. The number of women and girls playing cricket has increased markedly. Suddenly it wasn't just males who found cricket an enticing summer sports option.

55. In praise of Geoff Howarth

Much-maligned, much misunderstood New Zealand skipper

I want to say a word about Geoffrey Howarth, my first test captain, because I think he was one of the most misunderstood players of my time. The public perception of Geoff was that he was a casual, rather laid-back fellow, the typical English pro who didn't get too worked up about anything.

He wasn't like that at all. He was a classic stylist as a batsman, so during his peak years he made batting look very easy. He looked like he had a lot of time to play his shots and was always in control. When he was the New Zealand captain, he again seemed to have things well under control. He led New Zealand through many of their early great moments in the one-day arena and the public admired his coolness under pressure.

But it didn't come nearly as easy to Geoff as people might have thought. He was very prone to nerves and worried a great deal, especially before he had to go out to bat. Jeremy Coney talks about sitting next to him in the dressing room and seeing Geoff stroking his legs to try to calm himself down. He was even known to vomit with anxiety, but not a lot of substance because he seldom ate hearty meals on match day.

Once he was out on the field, he settled down well. Though Geoff's batting fell away near the end of his career — he got a real going-over in the West Indies in 1985 — he was always a very good captain, one of the best who led New Zealand in my time. I always enjoyed his captaincy. I know Martin Crowe and one or two of the others felt Geoff was too hard on them in their early years in the New Zealand team, but I never had those sorts of problems.

It wasn't easy for him, either. When he was the captain, we were involved in some long tours of Australia, with a huge number of one-day matches. He led the team in

News Media Auckland

Geoff Howarth (right) helps Stephen Boock with his field-placings. Let's not forget what a good captain Geoff was.

the days before there was a team coach, so a lot of responsibility fell on his shoulders. For a person prone to anxiety, it must have been especially gruelling.

Away from cricket, Geoff wasn't the most organised of people. It was a mistake when he was appointed the New Zealand coach after Wally Lees was sacked. It wasn't that Geoff lacked the knowledge, but to be a successful coach, he would have needed a very mature group of players and an exceptionally organised manager, because the discipline wasn't going to come from Geoff.

I believe he could well have been a much more successful international coach had he had more help around him. A John Graham/Geoff Howarth/Stephen Fleming management trio would have had a much more solid look about it.

Instead, Geoff's team contained an inordinate number of young players who were rather immature, plus some senior players with whom he did not get on especially well. It was a recipe for disaster and that's how his coaching stint turned out. It ended way before the expiry date on his contract.

It doesn't take away from what he did as a captain, though. He led New Zealand to a shock home-series triumph over the West Indies in 1980 and gave us the confidence to take on any team in the world with genuine belief that we could win.

He had a good balance as a captain. He wasn't averse to taking the odd risk, but he knew when to batten down the hatches and play tight. Because of the unsatisfactory way his time as New Zealand coach ended, there is perhaps a slight tendency to overlook his large contribution as a player and captain. That would be wrong.

The ability to read a game of cricket is a great asset. Geoff Howarth possessed it in good quantities. His dropping as a player was also viewed by some as untimely as it came at the end of the Caribbean tour of 1985. Ironically, too, it came after a gutsy 84 opening the batting against the fearsome foursome of Holding, Garner, Marshall and Davis.

Over the years I always felt he had a pretty good working relationship with Frank Cameron, the convenor of selectors and honorary coach, but it obviously got very strained around this time.

Footnote: Geoff Howarth has one unusual claim to fame. He appeared in an Ashes test match nearly three years before he made his test debut for New Zealand. In the early 1970s, Howarth went about forging a county career with Surrey. While living in London, he went to watch the fifth test of the 1972 England-Australia series, at the Oval, and agreed to fill the role of 13th man for England.

His good mate Bob Willis was 12th man, and Howarth agreed to help out. Normally a 13th man's activities would be fairly much restricted to carrying drinks and running errands. But there was one day at the Oval when Willis had to take the field to replace the injured John Snow. Soon after, the England captain, Ray Illingworth, also hurt himself. The England fieldsmen looked around at their dressing room and out trotted Geoff Howarth to field for England.

Up in the commentary box, Trevor Bailey looked at this youngster with the longish blond hair making his way out into the middle and said: 'I don't know who this is coming on now, but it looks like a girl.'

56. Revelatory batting gained little reward

Rodney Redmond — a one-test wonder

The Rodney Redmond story is one of the most bizarre — outrageous, even — in the history of New Zealand cricket. Redmond was a promising young cricketer in Wellington, a left-hand batsman and a left-arm spin bowler. I used to watch him when he was part of the Kilbirnie club team I followed as a lad.

In his second first-class match, for the New Zealand Under-23 team in 1966, he took 4–54 and 6–56 against Wellington. The next season he made 76 for Wellington against Les Favell's strong Australian team, so he was obviously a cricketer of ability.

Then Redmond moved to Auckland and developed into a punishing opening batsman. In 1972 he made his international debut, playing for New Zealand B in the Coca-Cola Cup one-day match against Victoria. Though New Zealand lost, Redmond batted so well that his 69 earned him the Man of the Match award. In the warm-up limited-over match against Victorian Universities, he had made 37.

The following season, Redmond was part of the New Zealand team that made a brief visit to Australia. He scored 49 and 38 retired hurt against a strong South Australian attack.

Back home, when Vic Pollard was unavailable for the third test against Pakistan because it was played on a Sunday, Redmond was chosen to make his test debut, regular opener Terry Jarvis dropping down the order to accommodate him.

Redmond's batting was a revelation. He smashed the Pakistanis all around Eden Park, at one stage hitting spinner Majid Khan for five successive boundaries. He reached his 50 in 79 minutes and was the dominant partner in a big opening stand with Glenn Turner. They raised the 100 in 90 hectic minutes. Redmond kept blazing

Rodney Redmond . . . what went wrong?

away and reached his century in 136 minutes, having hit 20 fours and a five. He became the third New Zealander to score a century on test debut.

So well did Redmond bat that day that there was something of a carnival atmosphere among the 15,000 spectators at Eden Park. Hundreds of people streamed on to the field to celebrate his century with him — twice in fact, because they mobbed him prematurely when he was on only 99.

He made 107 in that innings and when he followed it with another impressive knock of 56 in the second innings, it seemed a new batting star had emerged. Don

Cameron, writing in the *New Zealand Herald*, spoke of 'the drama, the breathtaking tension, the audacity of an innings that will remain a piece of Eden Park history'.

Naturally Redmond was chosen for the tour of England that northern summer. It was not a good experience for Redmond, though he began with innings of 65, 57, 79 and 11 not out. Eventually he played just 10 first-class games, making 483 runs at an average of 28.41. He played the two one-day internationals on the tour, but was not chosen for any of the tests.

When someone has batted as well in a test as Redmond did at Eden Park, he obviously has something special. It's worth persevering a bit with that sort of talent. Redmond felt that the tour hierarchy of Congdon, who was the captain, Turner and manager Jack Saunders treated him poorly. They must surely look back and wonder if they made the most of what Redmond had to offer, especially when John Parker, who opened in the three tests, totalled 23 runs for the series at an average of 4.60.

Years later Redmond, by then living in Perth, said: 'The tour was a very disillusioning experience for me. Once I got home I pretty well gave away top cricket. I had lost my enthusiasm.'

Redmond played only sporadically for Auckland after that, closing his first-class career with a century against Otago in 1976. He left test cricket having batted twice, for a century and a half-century, and with the Bradman-like average of 81.50.

He later moved to Perth and was lost to New Zealand cricket, though his son, Aaron, seems to have inherited his father's cricket ability. Aaron, who learned his cricket in Australia, has thrown in his lot with New Zealand and made his first-class debut for the South Island against the North in the 1999–2000 season and has played for Canterbury since. He has been a part of the New Zealand Cricket Academy, touring India in 2000 with an Academy side that also included such players as Kerry Walmsley, Jacob Oram, Lou Vincent, James Franklin, Hamish and James Marshall, Chris Martin and Andrew Penn. Redmond is a right-hand bat and a leg-spin bowler who is regarded as a test player in the making.

Let's hope he is treated better by New Zealand cricket officialdom than was his father.

57. Bouncers flew as pacemen boiled

Untimely tour announcement drew Windies' ire

For fast bowlers who were supposed to be over the hill, Charlie Griffith and Richard Edwards certainly gave New Zealand's batsmen a hot time of it during the test match at the Basin Reserve in 1969.

New Zealand seemed set for victory when they began their second innings 72 minutes before stumps on the third day. Having bowled out the West Indies for 148 in their second innings, New Zealand needed just 164 for victory.

There was one problem: just before the New Zealand second innings began, the West Indies team to tour England had been announced, and fast bowlers Wes Hall, Griffith and Edwards had all been dropped. To put it mildly, they weren't best pleased. A telegram giving details of the selection for England had arrived at the *Sports Round-Up* studios in Wellington, and host Keith Quinn had put the news on air immediately. His were the actions of a good newsman, but they didn't exactly help the New Zealand cause.

The West Indians heard their services had been dispensed with and were determined to show they'd been discarded too soon. Griffith and Edwards unleashed a bombardment of bouncers at the New Zealand top order and Glenn Turner, Bevan Congdon and Graham Dowling fell in quick succession. Bespectacled Bryan Yuile came in as nightwatchman — I'll bet he was excited to get that job — and umpires Mackintosh and Shortt directed West Indies captain Gary Sobers that his bowlers were not to aim the ball at the batsman's body.

New Zealand was mighty relieved to get to stumps at 40–3. The next day, the fire had gone from both the wicket and the West Indies bowlers and New Zealand

News Media Auckland

Charlie Griffith . . . don't get him angry.

carried on to a hard-fought six-wicket victory.

On the subject of inopportune ground announcements, there was a case in Wellington in 1977 that is humorous in retrospect, but wasn't so funny at the time. Wellington was playing Australia at the Basin Reserve and was involved in a last-afternoon run chase that looked especially promising. John Morrison was at the wicket and going well.

Suddenly, in those official tones that Wellington cricket and rugby patrons knew only too well, ground announcer David Grey asked for everyone's attention. He proceeded to tell spectators that the New Zealand team for the first test had been selected, and read out the names of the 12 players chosen. By a process of elimination, it wasn't hard to work out that one of the batsmen dropped was John Morrison, who'd been in the New Zealand side not long returned from the tour of India and Pakistan.

Morrison hadn't had a bad domestic season and was hopeful of retaining his test spot. The news was a real blow to him and learning about it while out in the middle trying to beat the Australians was hardly the best of times to hear it.

58. Jerry Coney, at your service

The case of the reluctant 12th man

The role of 12th man is seldom fondly regarded by those who have been so appointed. There are a number of reasons. Initially, of course, it's disappointing because if you're 'it', you've missed the playing eleven . . . missed the cut. It also means you're likely to be fairly busy acting out your role as nursemaid, butler, courier, messenger and often scapegoat during the course of the match.

I was fortunate. Selectors almost always name only one wicketkeeper in each 12 or 13-man squad, so if you get that far, you're going to get a game. I did, however, observe some rather unenthusiastic 12th men down the years.

Chief among these was Jeremy Coney. There may never have been a more reluctant Jeeves. He was a certainty in New Zealand cricket teams through from the late 1970s until his retirement in 1987. Therefore, unless he was given a game off in a touring situation, he seldom had the opportunity to perform the 12th man role.

In 1983 on the tour of England, Jerry was spelled along with a couple of others for the game against Hampshire in Bournemouth. As is always the case, the splinter bums gathered together relatively early to divvy up the duties, so all could get some time out and benefit from the breather. Jerry, as the senior, pulled rank and decided he would be on duty while New Zealand batted.

It is generally a sound theory: at most the 12th man is looking after only two players at a time and doesn't run the risk of having to spend a few hours substituting as a fieldsman.

Well, it's a sound theory, that is, if you're not waiting on a fussy batsman hell-bent on a long stay at the crease on a hot day.

News Media Auckland

Jeremy Coney indulges in a little underarm activity. He was never lost for a comical response.

Martin Crowe was a fussy batsman, often prone to long stays at the crease and on a hot day could often get very thirsty and require several changes of attire. He sweats a lot.

Picture this, then . . . Crowe at the wicket making plenty, Coney growing in frustration as the master batsman constantly calls for a change of gloves, a drink, a change of sweat bands, a change of head band, a fresh towel, a new shirt, some sun cream. Frustration grows as the Mantis repeatedly has to leg it out to the middle to answer each new demand about every 10 minutes.

Players in the dressing room quickly pick up on 'the game', as do umpires and players in the middle. It should be pointed out that in the case of the 12th man, the playing 11 always have right of way. They cannot be refused. Therefore Jerry continued to do his duty long into the afternoon. Finally, after he'd made so many visits that the crowd had become familiar with him and were laughing, he snapped.

At the next gesture of request from Crowe, there was a small delay until Coney burst from the dressing room and sprinted to the middle carrying the batsman's cricket bag (coffin) complete with all his playing attire and civilian clothes as well. Once in the middle he opened the lid of the coffin and proceeded to dump the whole bloody lot in the middle of the pitch (gloves, lip balm, cream, Crowe cosmetics, jock straps etc).

It was a brilliant reply — typical Coney. Even Crowe had to admit he had been upstaged for a minute or two. In the history of cricket it was one of the very rare occasions when a 12th man had received a greater ovation on his return to the pavilion than a well-performed star batsman.

It was okay in Bournemouth at a pinch, but wouldn't have been the done thing at Lord's, though you wouldn't put it past Coney.

Footnote: of all the intriguing choices for New Zealand team 12th man down the years, the most unusual may have occurred in 1936, when New Zealand met the MCC at the Basin Reserve. Henry Lubransky was the home team's 12th man. Lubransky had never played first-class cricket and never did. He was a keen Kilbirnie player and an extremely agile fieldsman. However, he had no pretensions to being either a batsman or bowler of first-class level.

The modern trend is for selectors to pick a squad of 12 or 13. Once they have cut this down to a playing 11, they will sometimes name a local player specifically as 12th man. Usually this person is an outstanding fieldsman. The New Zealand selectors of 1936 deserve congratulations for being decades ahead of their time.

Incidentally, Lubransky did eventually make his mark in sport. He went on to become chairman of the New Zealand Badminton Federation and his family have had a long involvement in that sport.

59. When the 'Truth' really does hurt

A newspaper column that fired a team

It's difficult to think of a stranger build-up to any of the 63 test matches in which I played than the goings-on in Christchurch before the test against the West Indies in March 1987. We hear a lot about psychology in sport these days and there are all sorts of theories about how to prepare a player and a team for a big match.

What went on in Christchurch gives lie to all that thinking because I doubt it would be possible to plan a worse preparation.

We went to Christchurch for the third test down 1–0 in the series. The West Indies was a good team. They were led by Viv Richards and had batting stars like Richards himself, Gordon Greenidge, Desmond Haynes, Richie Richardson — all among the world's best — plus useful performers in Larry Gomes and Gus Logie. They had a class wicketkeeper-batsman in Jeffrey Dujon and a fearsome pace bowling foursome of Malcolm Marshall, Joel Garner, Anthony Gray and Courtney Walsh. As their squad also included Carl Hooper, Michael Holding and Patrick Patterson, it can be seen this was not a team to be taken lightly.

And they were determined. They were proud of their hard-earned tag as the best team in the world and were acutely embarrassed that on their previous visit to New Zealand, in 1980, we'd beaten them in the test and one-day series. They were bent on extracting some revenge.

The series was one long, tough battle. In the first test, at Wellington, second innings centuries by John Wright and Martin Crowe earned us a good draw. They were far too good in the second test and won by 10 wickets, despite another Crowe century.

So to Christchurch for a must-win match. Between the second and third tests

Don Neely Collection

Richard Hadlee urges Ewen Chatfield to lead New Zealand from the field after one of the most bizarre days of my test career.

a Richard Hadlee column appeared in *Truth* newspaper, criticising us as a team for our sloppy practice habits and tardy attitude. This did not go down well with the boys. Such criticism should remain within the team. To air it publicly, especially at such a critical part of the series, was virtually unprecedented.

Then, in the dressing room before the game — the first day's play was lost to rain — Glenn Turner, our coach, raised the matter of the column. Perhaps he felt the issue needed to be discussed and then the whole business put to bed. Jeremy Coney, our captain, made his feelings clear. He felt that he and the team had been let down by Hadlee and said so strongly.

There was no doubt that Hadlee was obviously taken aback by the retort. It had been upfront and open, but still confined to the dressing room — the right forum.

Game time approached and Hadlee began to look increasingly wounded. Suddenly we faced the very real prospect of entering this vital match without our major weapon, Hadlee. It was as strange a situation as I can remember in the team dressing room. I always felt Richard would play, but I can't say I was 100 per cent sure about that. He was always so punctual and meticulous in his match-day preparations — the consummate pro, but that particular morning he was anything but. He was visibly upset.

There was some more talk, but positions began to firm and by the time we took the field, Coney and Hadlee weren't talking. Jeremy had won the toss and elected to field, always a good move against the West Indies of that era. They were typical Lancaster Park bowling conditions and we needed our big boys operating on all cylinders.

Our chief strike bowler took the new ball, as he always did, and Jeremy took his position at second slip, as he always did. Richard was not himself in that first spell. He had such a finely honed action that he very seldom bowled no-balls, but there were several in his first spell. After a few overs, he took himself off and marched off to gully, his preferred fielding slot.

Coney watched this and asked John Wright, who'd been acting as an intermediary between the pair, to check if Hadlee had finished his spell. Wright duly jogged down to gully, a distance of around 40 metres, to confirm the fact and was given the nod that in fact, yes, that was it. Any one of us fielding behind the wicket could have walked the 10 metres or so to do it, but the captain was determined to make a very open point.

Martin Snedden was summoned without warning from fine leg to take the ball and it must be said that he and Ewen Chatfield did a fantastic job against the best batting side in the world.

The unbelievable part is that with all this going on, we had a dream day. Chatfield bowled really well, knocking over Greenidge, Gomes and Richards cheaply. Then Hadlee came back and looked much more settled. He finished with 6–50 and — it's funny how these things work out — three of his wickets were the result of catches by Jeremy Vernon Coney. Celebrations between the two were very obviously muted — but our extraordinary success helped quell feelings a bit. It's not often such a strong batting lineup is bowled out in under three hours for just 100. By the end of the innings, Hadlee and Coney were even exchanging mild pleasantries at the fall of wickets.

It turned out to be a memorable match for New Zealand. We batted very positively and made 332–9 declared, then bowled them out for 264 and won by five wickets. Coney bowed out of test cricket in this match, so I was pleased he finished on a high. I am sure, though, that when he recalls the game, it is with mixed emotions.

I'm pleased to say Jeremy and Richard are on better terms these days. Richard joined Jeremy in the commentary box during the 1990s, often in his role as a Bank of New Zealand Cricket ambassador, and they formed a good team. They've continued to see a lot of each other since Richard became the convenor of the national selection panel.

It should be remembered Jeremy was very much a part of the anti-Hadlee faction during the infamous 'Alfa-Romeo — keep the car' episode a few years earlier. But that's another outrageous story . . .

60. Doing the damage at No 11

World record stand is highlight for Collinge

Richard Collinge was one of the cricketers I used to look up to when I was a boy. To a primary school lad hanging around the Kilbirnie clubrooms on a Saturday, Collinge was a fearsome sight. He looked about 9 ft tall and just about as broad, had a tremendously long run with a terrifying leap at the end, and seemed to deliver one thunderbolt after another.

I often used to think how pleased I was that I didn't have to face him, and I don't think many club batsmen in Wellington looked forward to the Saturday confrontation with Collinge very eagerly. The alternative wasn't so flash either, because he had a good mate in Mike Coles at the other end.

Collinge went on to play 35 tests for New Zealand and to take 116 test wickets. For a while he held the New Zealand record for most test wickets. That was before Richard Hadlee came along and put the mark beyond reach, possibly forever.

As well as three times taking five wickets in an innings in tests, Collinge also bowled one of the most famous deliveries in New Zealand test cricket. It was at the Basin Reserve in February 1978, when he clean bowled England captain Geoff Boycott for a duck and set New Zealand on the way to their first-ever win over their oldest test rival. I'll never forget that delivery. It was a bit breezy and there was a cloud of dust as Boycott tried to dig out the classic yorker. Boycott hated it then and hates the memory just as much now. It's a wonderful tool to shut him up in the commentary box from time to time. Other memories from that test include:

John Wright on debut nicking the first delivery of the match to Bob Taylor and being given not out by Bob Monteith — Wrighty never looked back.

Every tailender's dream . . . Richard Collinge set a batting world record.

Stephen Boock's mercurial run out from side on of Bob Taylor, a truly great piece of cricket.

The smile on Jumbo Anderson's face on the completion of that famous victory, a smile that to this day has never disappeared, although often masked by a gin and a white owl.

Anyway I digress . . . back to the man in question.

For all Collinge's great bowling for his country, his most cherished moment in test cricket came as a batsman. Most bowlers fancy themselves a bit with the bat and I've found the fast bowlers especially like to hammer the ball. Collinge was a bit more cultured than that. He played some good club innings and was quite an orthodox batsman. Like a surprising number of players, he batted right-handed even though he bowled with his left. Bryan Yuile, Gary Troup, David Sewell, John Morrison, Murray Chapple and Stephen Boock are others I can quickly recall who also did that.

When New Zealand played Pakistan at Eden Park in February 1973, Collinge and Brian Hastings put on 151 runs for the 10th wicket, a world record for test cricket. Hastings was finally dismissed for 110 and Collinge was left not out 68 and telling his team-mates that Hastings' dismissal had cost him a certain test century.

It was a remarkable test match. Pakistan batted first and made 402 with Majid Khan making a century. Despite Rodney Redmond's blazing debut test 107 and his first wicket partnership with Glenn Turner of 159, New Zealand crumbled to 251–9 in the face of Intikhab's leg-spin and googlies. When Collinge walked out to join Hastings, New Zealand had not even avoided the follow on. The pair proceeded to put on 100 at better than even time and the Pakistanis, growing increasingly frustrated, began to panic and put down some chances. Hastings and Collinge batted from lunch until after tea. When New Zealand's total had equalled Pakistan's, Hastings was bowled by Wasim Raja.

The 151 Hastings and Collinge added for the last wicket (in 155 minutes) beat the previous test record for the 10th wicket of 130, set by Tip Foster and Wilfred Rhodes nearly 70 years earlier. Collinge and Hastings still hold that world record, though they now share it jointly with Pakistan's Azhar Mahmood and Mushtaq Ahmed, who added 151 runs for the 10th wicket, against South Africa at Rawalpindi in 1997.

Collinge's 68 included a six and six fours and is still the highest score in tests by a No 11.

Incidentally, New Zealanders have four times been involved in century-plus stands for the last wicket. Besides Collinge-Hastings, there have been 124 by John Bracewell and Stephen Boock at Sydney in 1985, 118 by Nathan Astle and Chris Cairns against England on that madcap afternoon in Christchurch in 2002 and 106 (undefeated) by Astle and Danny Morrison against England at Auckland in 1997, when they saved the test.

61. Astle's innings crafted in Jade

The quickest double-century in test history

Has there ever been a more outrageous innings than Nathan Astle's never-to-be forgotten 222 against England at Christchurch in March 2002? It was the most breathtaking, astonishing display of hitting imagineable.

I've seen some big hitting in my time. Just restricting myself to New Zealand players, Lance and Chris Cairns and Richard Hadlee have played some incredibly powerful innings. There's always been big hitting. John Reid, Bruce Taylor, Dick Motz . . . we've produced plenty.

But nothing approaches what Astle did in Christchurch. Perhaps the most remarkable thing about Astle's innings was how he kept it going. This wasn't a case of one blazing over and then out, or even a smashing half-century. Astle tore England apart for nearly four hours.

He's not a big man, not in the Dick Motz-Lance Cairns-Chris Cairns mould. But he's a mighty clubber of the ball. We'd seen it before in some blazing one-day innings all over the world, but never anything like this, and certainly not in a test.

In the commentary box at Jade Stadium, we were mentally beginning to pack up and direct our thoughts towards the next test, in Wellington, at about the time Astle really got going. After all, New Zealand needed an impossible 550 to win the match. He came in at 119–3, and when Adam Parore was dismissed, it was 252–6. Daniel Vettori, Chris Drum, Ian Butler and a lame Chris Cairns were the only batsmen left to support Astle.

But on this day, nothing could stop him. It didn't matter that the England attack included Matthew Hoggard, who'd taken 7–63 in the first innings, or the lively Andy Caddick, or medium-pacer Andy Flintoff or left-arm spinner Ashley

Giles. They could do nothing to stem the flow.

Suddenly the records started to tumble. Astle's innings was full of wonderful hitting, but it wasn't crude. He cut, glanced, hooked, drove. He didn't resort to crossbat swipes.

I suppose the one statistic that really spells out the breathtaking quality of his inning is that he reached his double-century off just 153 balls. A few weeks earlier Australian Adam Gilchrist had set a world record for the fastest test double-century, when he'd hammered 200 off 212 balls against South Africa at Johannesburg. Astle beat that record by a staggering margin of 59 balls. Before Gilchrist came along, Ian Botham held the record. He'd taken 220 balls to bring up his double-ton against India at the Oval in 1982.

Just think of it. It was the 1594th test match, in which there had been more than 54,000 innings, yet Astle's was 30 per cent better than any test innings ever played. Here's an abbreviated statistical breakdown of what he did that day in Christchurch:

- 50 in 74 minutes, from 54 balls, 10 fours
- 100 in 148 minutes, from 114 balls, 16 fours and two sixes
- 150 in 185 minutes, from 136 balls, 25 fours and three sixes
- 200 in 217 minutes, from 153 balls, 27 fours and nine sixes
- 222 in 231 minutes, from 168 balls, 28 fours and 11 sixes

It was the most exhilarating sustained piece of batting ever seen in a test match. England were not forced, as they would have been in limited-over cricket, to have restrictions on their fielding placements. They were able to place everyone around the boundary's edge. Their bowlers were permitted to deliver the ball much wider than they would be in a one-dayer.

But it made no difference to Astle. He jetted from 101 to 200 in 69 minutes off 39 balls. He made the ground we used to call Lancaster Park look like a postage stamp as he stepped inside and hooked the pace bowlers, or drove them over the boundary.

Astle and Cairns added 118 for the last wicket in 55 minutes. Cairns scored 23 of them. How often would Cairns, scoring at nearly a run a ball, be so overshadowed?

Twice Astle hit balls onto the roofs of the stands at Jade Stadium. One of those hits, an off-drive, was as big a hit as I've seen on a cricket field. In terms of time, his was the second fastest double-century ever, three minutes behind the record set by one Donald Bradman at Leeds in 1930. In fairness to Astle, it should be stated that if he hadn't hit those two balls onto the roof and caused long delays while replacements were found, he'd have had that record, too. In addition, cricket was played at a much faster clip in 1930. Back then it was nothing to see 125 overs bowled in a six-hour day. Now bowlers can't get through 90 in that time. It's estimated that Bradman raised his double-century that day off about 260 deliveries.

Astle set all sorts of records. His 11 sixes was a New Zealand test record, beating

Nathan Astle blasting away during one of the most fantastic innings in test cricket history.

by two the previous mark of nine, held by Chris Cairns, and only one off Wasim Akram's all-time mark of 12. Hoggard's first two overs with the second new ball cost 41 runs; Caddick went for 25 in one frenetic over.

At one point, Astle hit Caddick for seven successive boundaries — 4, 6, 6, 4, 6, 6, 6. He smashed eight consecutive Hoggard deliveries for 4, 2, 4, 4, 4, 6, 2, 4. From 4 p.m. until 4.35 p.m., Astle scored 80 runs off 24 balls. He personally scored 10 or more runs off 11 separate overs during his innings. No wonder there was a carnival atmosphere at the ground.

When Astle was finally out, caught behind by James Foster off Hoggard after about the only uncouth shot in his entire stay, New Zealand were dismissed for 451. They lost by 98 runs, but theirs was the second-biggest fourth innings total in test history.

I liked the way Lynn McConnell described Astle's innings. He said it was cricket's equivalent of Bob Beamon's long jump world record. Beamon's long jump record, set in 1968, was so outstanding it endured until 1991. Astle's double-century record may well last even longer.

Those present all felt the same about Astle's innings. Here's a sample of what others wrote:

The Sunday Times: 'Arguably, there has never been another match like it. Such was the mayhem wrought by Nathan Astle in perhaps the most remarkable display of calculated hitting ever seen at this level that another hour of carnage from his bat — and an hour of the day remained when he was out — might have been enough to steal for New Zealand one of the greatest victories in test history.

'Given that New Zealand still required 249 to win when their eighth wicket fell — and nobody was sure that the injured Chris Cairns would even come out to bat — it sounds preposterous to say such a thing. But it was the case. When it comes to Astle's knock, the figures speak for themselves.'

The Observer: 'For many, Astle's stunning hitting overshadowed the result. . .'

The Independent on Sunday: 'England outplayed New Zealand for all but an hour of this test to go 1–0 up in the series. But those 60 minutes, when Nathan Astle laid waste to England's attack, may yet have the greatest bearing on how this three-match series ends. When your best bowlers are treated like golf balls at a driving range, a gnawing fallibility works its way in.'

Sunday Mirror: 'One of the greatest innings in the history of cricket by Nathan Astle couldn't deny England victory in this crazy test match. Nasser Hussain's men held their nerve as Astle smashed his way into the record books. Astle's fightback as New Zealand chased a target of 550 for what would have been the greatest victory of all time made England sweat before he edged Matthew Hoggard to wicketkeeper James Foster.'

Sunday People: 'Nathan Astle set the Jade Stadium alight . . . Astle went berserk after passing his century with his second hundred coming off just 39 deliveries with Andy Caddick twice hit out of the ground.'

The Sunday Telegraph (Sydney): 'Ian Botham's record for the fastest double-century in test cricket lasted 20 years before Australia's Adam Gilchrist beat it. Gilchrist lasted only three weeks at the top. Yesterday in Christchurch, New Zealand's Nathan Astle didn't just trump Gilchrist's record, he obliterated it with a brutal assault on the England attack. It was a brilliant display, albeit too late to alter the result of the match, but it did ensure the margin of defeat was respectable.'

Reuters: 'Nathan Astle made England twitch with a record-breaking 222 as New Zealand fought to get 550 runs for victory in the first test. While the chase for the mammoth winning total was in vain, Astle's maelstrom of an innings beat Australian Adam Gilchrist's record for the fastest double-century recorded in Johannesburg three weeks ago.'

In the days after the match, a limited edition signed photo (a print run of 222) of Astle batting was sold. A television programme was compiled about Astle's innings and he became the subject of a video.

Astle's innings was the highest in test history by a player on the losing side and the second highest ever (behind George Headley's 223 in 1930) in the fourth innings of a test. He is the only New Zealander to have scored 200 runs in one day in test cricket.

Martin Crowe and Mark Nicholas of England called the last hour and a half of the innings live. Like Astle they were in 'the zone' in terms of their commentary and afterwards just like the batsman himself they were dazed, drained but thrilled to be a part of it.

Indeed, anyone who was at Jade Stadium that day, watched on TV, or listened on radio, or even read about the innings in newspapers, was in no doubt about its quality.

Therefore, like many New Zealanders I was stunned by *Wisden's* outrageous ranking of it as the 62nd best test innings of all time.

In 2000, *Wisden* produced a list of the top 100 test innings in test history. The innings were based on all sorts of factors — quality of opposition, state of the match, state of the pitch, length of innings and so on.

Don Bradman topped the list with his match-winning (and ultimately series-winning) 270 against England at Melbourne in 1936. *Wisden*, employing its complex points system, gave Bradman 262.35 points out of a possible 300 for that innings.

When Astle's innings was analysed, the *Wisden* adjudicators gave him 195.92 points, which would have placed him 60th on their original list, and now had him at 62nd (Inzamam-ul-Haq and Mark Butcher had played top 60-ranking innings after the original list was compiled).

I know that Astle's innings was played when his team were in a hopeless position, so therefore it did not alter the result of the test. But I would still rate it far higher than 62nd.

If you scan the list of the top 100 and ask how many innings will be talked about years or decades later, the honest answer is not that many. Astle's innings will never be forgotten. It was the innings of a lifetime, or maybe even of a century.

More Astle fireworks.

The 'Wisden' top 100 (issued in 2000)

Name	Score	For	Against	Venue	Season	Wisden Rating
1 Don Bradman	270	Australia	England	Melbourne	1936–37	262.4
2 Brian Lara	153*	West Indies	Australia	Bridgetown	1998–99	255.2
3 Graham Gooch	154*	England	West Indies	Headingley	1991	252.0
4 Ian Botham	149*	England	Australia	Headingley	1981	240.8
5 Don Bradman	299*	Australia	South Africa	Adelaide	1931–32	236.8
6 V.V.S. Laxman	281	India	Australia	Calcutta	2000–01	234.8
7 Clem Hill	188	Australia	England	Melbourne	1897–98	234.2
8 Azhar Mahmood	132	Pakistan	South Africa	Durban	1997–98	232.6
9 Kim Hughes	100*	Australia	West Indies	Melbourne	1981–82	229.7
10 Brian Lara	375	West Indies	England	St John's	1993–94	228.1
11 Reginald Foster	287	England	Australia	Sydney	1993–94	226.7
12 Clyde Walcott	220	West Indies	England	Bridgetown	1953–54	223.0
13 Mark Taylor	144	Australia	West Indies	St John's	1990–91	221.4
14 Brian Lara	213	West Indies	Australia	Kingston	1998–99	221.3
15 Dean Jones	184*	Australia	England	Sydney	1986–87	220.9
16 Salim Malik	237	Pakistan	Australia	Rawalpindi	1994–95	219.9
17 Pelham Warner	132*	England	South Africa	Johannesburg	1898–99	218.4
17 Reg Simpson	156*	England	Australia	Melbourne	1950–51	218.4
19 Hanif Mohammad	337	Pakistan	West Indies	Bridgetown	1957–58	217.3
20 John Edrich	310*	England	New Zealand	Headingley	1965	217.1
21 Gordon Greenidge	214*	West Indies	England	Lord's	1984	216.2
22 Mark Waugh	116	Australia	South Africa	Port Elizabeth	1996–97	215.7
23 Warwick Armstrong	159*	Australia	South Africa	Johannesburg	1902–03	212.9
24 Ijaz Ahmed	137	Pakistan	Australia	Sydney	1995–96	211.9
25 Ian Redpath	159*	Australia	New Zealand	Auckland	1973–74	210.5
26 Greg Chappell	182*	Australia	West Indies	Sydney	1975–76	209.9
27 Jackie McGlew	255*	South Africa	New Zealand	Wellington	1952–53	209.3
28 Clive Lloyd	161*	West Indies	India	Calcutta	1983–84	208.3
29 David Houghton	266	Zimbabwe	Sri Lanka	Bulawayo	1994–95	208.1
30 Dilip Vengsarkar	102*	India	England	Headingley	1986	206.9
31 Jeffrey Dujon	139	West Indies	Australia	Perth	1984–85	205.3
32 Charles Bannerman	165*	Australia	England	Melbourne	1876–77	205.1
33 Gary Sobers	365*	West Indies	Pakistan	Kingston	1957–58	204.6
33 George Bonnor	128	Australia	England	Sydney	1984–85	204.6
35 Dave Nourse	93*	South Africa	England	Johannesburg	1905–06	204.4
36 Gilbert Jessop	104	England	Australia	the Oval	1902	203.8
36 Don Bradman	103*	Australia	England	Melbourne	1932–33	203.8
38 Gundappa Viswanath	97*	India	West Indies	Madras (Chennai)	1974–75	203.1
39 Gordon Greenidge	213	West Indies	New Zealand	Auckland	1986–87	203.0
40 Graeme Pollock	274	South Africa	Australia	Durban	1969–70	202.9
41 Stan McCabe	232	Australia	England	Trent Bridge	1938	202.4
42 Faoud Bacchus	250	West Indies	India	Kanpur	1978–79	202.2
43 Saeed Anwar	188*	Pakistan	India	Calcutta	1998–99	201.9
44 Steve Waugh	200	Australia	West Indies	Kingston	1994–95	201.6
45 Neil Harvey	167	Australia	England	Melbourne	1958–59	201.5
46 Allan Border	163	Australia	India	Melbourne	1985–86	201.4
47 Don Bradman	334	Australia	England	Headingley	1930	201.1
48 Len Hutton	364	England	Australia	the Oval	1938	200.4
49 Gordon Greenidge	226	West Indies	Australia	Bridgetown	1990–91	199.8

50 Michael Slater	123	Australia	England	Sydney	1998–99	199.1
51 Basil Butcher	209*	West Indies	England	Trent Bridge	1966	198.8
52 Greg Chappell	204	Australia	India	Sydney	1980–81	198.7
53 Denis Amiss	179	England	India	Delhi	1976–77	198.4
54 Jack Ryder	201*	Australia	England	Adelaide	1924–25	198.3
55 Frank Worrell	191*	West Indies	England	Trent Bridge	1957	198.1
56 Arthur Morris	196	Australia	England	the Oval	1948	197.0
57 Kepler Wessels	173	Australia	West Indies	Sydney	1984–85	196.7
58 Gary Kirsten	275	South Africa	England	Durban	1999–00	196.2
59 George Headley	270*	West Indies	England	Kingston	1934–35	196.1
60 Len Hutton	205*	England	West Indies	Kingston	1953–54	195.6
61 Peter May	112	England	South Africa	Lord's	1955	195.6
62 Greg Chappell	176	Australia	New Zealand	Christchurch	1981–82	194.6
62 Lawrence Rowe	302	West Indies	England	Bridgetown	1973–74	194.6
64 Saeed Anwar	118	Pakistan	South Africa	Durban	1997–98	194.3
65 Bryan Young	267*	New Zealand	Sri Lanka	Dunedin	1996–97	193.9
65 Hanif Mohammad	187*	Pakistan	England	Lord's	1967	193.9
67 Colin Cowdrey	102	England	Australia	Melbourne	1954–55	193.8
68 Jack Lyons	134	Australia	England	Sydney	1891–92	193.6
69 Joe Darling	160	Australia	England	Sydney	1897–98	193.5
69 Viv Richards	182*	West Indies	England	Bridgetown	1980–81	193.5
71 Peter Burge	160	Australia	England	Headingley	1964	193.3
71 Derek Randall	150	England	Australia	Sydney	1978–79	193.3
73 David Gower	154*	England	West Indies	Kingston	1980–81	193.2
74 Sunil Gavaskar	221	India	England	the Oval	1979	192.9
75 Walter Hammond	336*	England	New Zealand	Auckland	1932–33	192.8
75 Kapil Dev	129	India	South Africa	Port Elizabeth	1992–93	192.8
77 Seymour Nurse	258	West Indies	New Zealand	Christchurch	1968–69	192.5
78 Allan Lamb	137*	England	New Zealand	Trent Bridge	1983	192.2
78 Clive Lloyd	129	West Indies	Australia	Brisbane	1968–69	192.2
80 Viv Richards	192*	West Indies	India	Delhi	1974–75	192.1
81 Peter May	104	England	Australia	Sydney	1954–55	192.0
82 Gundappa Viswanath	114	India	Australia	Melbourne	1980–81	191.9
83 Allan Border	115	Australia	England	Perth	1979–80	191.8
84 Graham Gooch	333	England	India	Lord's	1990	191.6
84 Kepler Wessels	162	Australia	England	Brisbane	1982–83	191.6
86 Water Hammond	231*	England	Australia	Sydney	1936–37	191.4
87 Bob Cowper	165	Australia	India	Sydney	1967–68	190.9
88 Mohammad Azharuddin	152	India	Sri Lanka	Ahmedabad	1993–94	190.6
89 Denis Amiss	262*	England	West Indies	Kingston	1973–74	190.4
90 Water Hammond	251	England	Australia	Sydney	1928–29	189.9
91 Mahela Jayawardene	242	Sri Lanka	India	Colombo	1998–99	189.5
91 Gary Kirsten	100*	South Africa	Pakistan	Faisalabad	1997–98	189.5
93 Geoff Boycott	191	England	Australia	Headingley	1977	189.1
94 Rohan Kanhai	217	West Indies	Pakistan	Lahore	1958–59	188.1
95 Viv Richards	291	West Indies	England	the Oval	1976	188.4
96 Sunil Gavaskar	236*	India	West Indies	Madras (Chennai)	1983–84	188.2
97 Victor Trumper	159	Australia	South Africa	Melbourne	1910–11	187.9
97 Don Bradman	103	Australia	England	Headingley	1938	187.9
99 Clem Hill	160	Australia	England	Adelaide	1907–08	187.6
100 Dudley Nourse	208	South Africa	England	Trent Bridge	1951	186.9

While on the subject of the *Wisden* top 100, let me state categorically that it's outrageous only one New Zealand innings was deemed worthy — Bryan Young's 267 not out at Carisbrook in 1997. Players before my time talk of Bert Sutcliffe's heroic 80 not out against South Africa in 1952, Mark Burgess' series-winning 119 not out against Pakistan at Dacca in 1969 and John Reid's 100 (out of 159) against England at Lancaster Park in 1963.

I saw several truly magnificent innings by Martin Crowe, listened to Glenn Turner's twin centuries against Australia at Lancaster Park in 1974, and to Bevan Congdon's gutsy 176 against England at Trent Bridge in 1973. Bruce Edgar, Chris Cairns and others have played memorable innings.

The greatest fighting display might well have been Mark Greatbatch's 146 not out against Australia at Perth in 1989. We trailed by 290 runs on the first innings and were 11–2 in the second innings, but Paddy defied Alderman, Lawson, Rackermann, Hughes and Moody for 655 minutes to save the match.

It's ridiculous to think that even Greatbatch's brave effort didn't make the top 100. In such circumstances, you have to question the judgement of those compiling the list.

New Zealand fared better in the bowling. Richard Hadlee's 9–52 against Australia at Brisbane in 1985 is rated the fifth all-time best performance. Curiously, Hugh Tayfield's 9–113 against England in 1957 ranked above the 10-wicket hauls of Anil Kumble and Jim Laker, so it wasn't just New Zealanders who had cause to lift an eyebrow when the lists were released.

62. To Victor always went the spoils

Trumper was always a thorn in our side

Champion Australian batsman Victor Trumper was said to be a gentle soul, and was one of the most popular cricketers in the world in the early years of the 20th century. But even the affable Trumper must have tried the patience of New Zealand's leading bowlers while helping his teams impose two of the most mammoth defeats in our cricket history.

At Sydney in February 1899, New Zealand lost to New South Wales by an innings and 384 runs, still our heaviest-ever loss.

Trumper thrashed the New Zealand attack, scoring 253 in 330 minutes. New South Wales scored 588 and New Zealand were bowled out for 140 and 66. It was a pretty good New Zealand bowling attack, too, with such well-rated bowlers as Alex Downes, Frank Frankish, Ernie Upham, Arthur Fisher and Dan Reese. Frankish generously dropped Trumper twice in one over off his own bowling, and Trumper thanked him in no uncertain terms.

Trumper was at it again when Australia stopped off in New Zealand on their way to England in 1905. In the second international, at the Basin Reserve, he smashed 172 in not much more than two hours. Australia made 593–9 declared and New Zealand could reply with only 94 and 141. Australia won by an innings and 358 runs.

That wasn't the end of Trumper gorging himself on New Zealand bowlers, either. In early 1914, he toured New Zealand with a team of Australians put together by wealthy New Zealand businessman Arthur Sims. The visiting team ran up some colossal scores against various provincial rep teams. When Sims' side played South Canterbury, they smashed their way to 922–9 declared in just 330 minutes. Jack

News Media Auckland

Victor Trumper . . . the scourge of early New Zealand teams.

Crawford hammered 354 and Trumper made 137. The pair added 293 in 69 minutes!

Against Canterbury, the Australians made 653, with Trumper (293) and Sims (184 not out) adding 433 runs in the three hours Trumper was at the wicket.

New Zealanders were fortunate to have this extended view of one of the game's legendary batsman. Trumper carried on in the same manner all over New Zealand, delighting cricket lovers everywhere. No one would have guessed then that the following year this most popular of players would be dead.

Cricket being the game it is, there will inevitably be occasions when one team underperforms and suffers a heavy defeat. We think of New Zealand's big loss to

Australia at the Basin Reserve in 1946, and the infamous match at Eden Park in 1955, when New Zealand were bowled out for 26 in their second innings, turning a possible victory into an innings loss. There were some less-than-memorable test performances during New Zealand's 1958 tour of England, when top-class England bowlers such as Frank Tyson, Brian Statham, Fred Trueman, Trevor Bailey, Jim Laker and Tony Lock wrought havoc in helpful conditions.

I was involved in some nightmarish days myself. In terms of test cricket, we had back-to-back losses inside three days in Australia in 1980. Thinking of one-dayers, there was a humiliating one-dayer at the Basin Reserve in 1982 when we were bowled out for 74 in 29 overs and Australia won by eight wickets, with 30 overs and most of the day to spare. There was also the match in Sharjah in 1990 when we were again bowled out for 74 and Pakistan passed our total in no time for the loss of just two wickets.

Another heavy defeat I recall well took place in Berbice, Guyana, in 1985. Berbice is a town less than an hour's flight from Georgetown and to get there we were shuttled over in light aircraft and helicopters. The ground had been oversold and disgruntled patrons who could not get in lit a fire outside in the direction of the wind, so that thick smoke blew across the ground. They seemed to feel if they couldn't watch the cricket, then they would do their best to stop it altogether.

Desmond Hayes, as he did so often that season, scored heavily. He batted through the West Indies innings and made 145 not out in their innings of 259–5. In reply, we batted disastrously. Lance Cairns had a bash at the end and made 33; otherwise no one could score more than 20 and we were all out for 129. Eldine Baptiste, the least imposing of all the fearsome West Indies fast bowlers, caused us the most problems that day, taking 2–18 from seven overs.

There was a strange end to the match. Planes could not land at night at Berbice, so it was imperative the cricketers got back to Georgetown as quickly as possible. Players whose involvement in the match was over — our top-order — therefore were flown back as soon as possible. This led to the bizarre circumstance of the lower-order batsmen continuing the game and having their team-mates flying overhead on their way out — the airport was next to the cricket ground. It wasn't a memorable match in terms of the result, but it was certainly an unusual one.

63. Murray's catch was pick of Pakistani bunch

How Bruce bagged a beaut . . . with a banana in one hand

Bruce Murray was a player who caught my attention at an early age. He was one of the stars of the Wellington team when I was growing up and many a time I watched him walk out to open the batting with Grahame Bilby. I was intrigued by Murray's initials. Newspapers recorded him as BAG Murray, which I found fascinating.

I've since learned that he is Bruce Alexander Grenfell Murray and that his teammates called him Bags for obvious reasons.

Like Bryan Yuile and Vic Pollard, he wouldn't play cricket on Sundays because of his religious beliefs, which eventually cost him his test place.

Murray had a good batting average of 37.27 for New Zealand. Much more impressive was his test bowling average of 0.00. He took one wicket, that of Abid Ali, with his leg-spinners and never conceded a run. Imagine that: fated always to be at the top of New Zealand's test bowling averages!

But the best story about this unusual cricketer concerns the time he took a catch in a test match while clutching a banana. It happened at Dacca, Pakistan, in 1969. He was fielding on the third man boundary and became increasingly irate at being pelted with all manner of missiles by bored spectators. When he was hit by a banana, it was too much, even for someone as mild-tempered as Bruce.

He picked up the offending piece of fruit and marched towards the wicket to complain to his captain, Graham Dowling. The umpire belatedly saw him coming and tried to prevent Dayle Hadlee from bowling the next ball to Asif Iqbal. Hadlee could not stop himself and bowled it short.

Sensing from the umpire's agitation that something was amiss, Iqbal sliced it to

News Media Auckland

Bruce Murray . . . not a banana in sight.

deep gully, where Murray had arrived. 'Might as well catch it,' thought Murray, so he dived and made a beautiful catch, emerging with ball in one hand and banana unscathed in the other.

Iqbal was naturally enough given not out and Bruce very soon saw the humour of the situation.

There have been other great fruit and vege stories in cricket. What about this one, which happened during a Taranaki v Hawke's Bay Hawke Cup elimination match at Pukekura Park:

When the first ball after the break was sent down, there was one problem — it wasn't a cricket ball at all, but a juicy red tomato. Doug Morland, the batsman, blocked most things and the tomato got the full face treatment. The fielding side were in the know and fell about the place in stitches.

Morland, cool as you like, on completion of cleaning the face of his bat, looked up to the bowler's umpire and simply asked: 'Sir, how many vegetables to come in the over?'

Ironically Morland, though he played first-class cricket for only a short time, developed the nickname of 'The Pear Shaped Cricketer'.

64. Most famous deliveries

The dozen most famous deliveries in New Zealand cricket

1. Trevor Chappell's underarm, Melbourne Cricket Ground, 1981.

2. Geoff Boycott bowled by Richard Collinge to set up New Zealand's first win over England, Basin Reserve, 1978.

3. Don Bradman, c Eric Tindill, b Jack Cowie, 11, the only time Bradman played against New Zealand, Adelaide Oval, 1937.

4. Stephen Boock's match-winning leg-bye off Joel Garner, earning New Zealand a one-wicket win over the West Indies, Carisbrook, 1980.

5. Lance Cairns hits Dennis Lillee for a one-handed six, Melbourne Cricket Ground, 1983.

6. Ewen Chatfield almost dies after being hit by a Peter Lever delivery, Eden Park, 1975.

7. Ken Wadsworth's cover drive off Greg Chappell to win New Zealand's first test against Australia, Lancaster Park, 1974.

8. Everton Weekes, c Noel McGregor, b Jack Alabaster to seal New Zealand's first test victory, Eden Park, 1956.

9. Arun Lal, c Chris Kuggeleijn, b Richard Hadlee, giving Hadlee the world record for test wickets, Bangalore, 1988.

Don Neely Collection

The Ken Wadsworth drive that is as vivid today as it was in 1974.

10. Intikhab Alam, c Geoff Howarth, b Peter Petherick, the third victim in the only hat-trick taken in test cricket by a New Zealander, Gaddafi Stadium, Lahore, 1976.

11. Charmaine Maston is c Rebecca Rolls, b Clare Nicholson and New Zealand win the women's World Cup in the last over of the final, Brierley Oval, Christchurch, 2000.

12. Martin Crowe, c Tillakaratne, b Ranatunga 299 when a test triple-century seemed assured, Basin Reserve, 1991.

65. Poms plastered

None more satisfying than the '84 win over England

When I think of the various test victories I was part of, the most outrageous might well have been our win over England at Lancaster Park in March 1984.

We beat them by an innings and 132 runs! They never reached 100 in either innings! We needed just one minute over two days to do the job! We made England follow on, the first time we'd done that in more than half a century of test cricket! What a fun week that was. It wasn't the worst England team, either. David Gower, Allan Lamb, Ian Botham, Mike Gatting, Bob Taylor and Bob Willis formed the core of what should have been a good team.

But when they got to Christchurch for the second test, the first having been drawn, they were right grumpy. They didn't like the look of the pitch, and to be fair there had been some criticism of its variable bounce during the season.

They're called tests for a reason, however. They're supposed to test players. England didn't seem to want to be tested that week. Geoffrey Howarth won the toss and batted, and it's fair to say we struggled. I can say without fear of contradiction that there weren't too many batsmen on our side overjoyed at the prospect of batting, especially after witnessing the behaviour of one early Willis delivery, in particular. Bowling from the southern end, he charged in with his unique style, pitched one short of a length which reared over John Wright's head at an acute angle and easily cleared keeper Taylor down to the fence for four byes.

Now, it is the norm for most top-order batsmen to field in the cordon around the keeper and slips area, and an immediate meeting took place between Messrs Lamb, Botham, Gower and Gatting. It was at about that point I would imagine that we began to get the ascendancy.

Norman Cowans, Bob Willis and Tony Pigott, called into the side to cover for injuries, had an enjoyable time of it, making the ball seam and cut, and getting plenty of lift. But they bowled erratically; their length was all over the place.

Our batsmen fought hard and everyone seemed especially eager to play strokes. Perhaps they felt they weren't going to be in too long, so they would prosper while they could. Jeff Crowe scored 47 from 73 balls and Jerry Coney 41 from 79. We got to 137–5.

Then, on his home ground, out walked Richard Hadlee. If those before him had played extravagantly, he batted like a millionaire, slashing, driving, pulling. He'd back away and poke the ball through gully, or he'd step into it and whack it over mid-wicket, or he'd go inside it and flick it round the corner. Richard batted only 111 minutes and faced just 81 balls, but in that time he produced a sensational 99.

His innings must have been the ultimate in frustration for the England team. He hit 18 boundaries, but in between them were air shots, wafts, edges. He'd leave his stumps exposed and get away with it. It was, in short, an outrageous innings. It was also a match-winning effort.

I had my head down that season. I'd fought my way back into the New Zealand team and was determined to hold my place. I got to 32 not out in the relatively sedate (for me) time of 85 minutes.

Batting at the other end to Richard was very exciting. Here was a talented player riding his luck. He was finally out nicking one to Taylor off Willis when he needed just one for his century.

In the end we finished with 307, a useful total on a wicket that Hadlee later described as a 'minefield'. But we could never have guessed how England would capitulate.

They were bowled out for 82 (in three hours) and 93 (again in three hours). Our bowlers had a picnic. Hadlee, of course, was the greediest, picking up eight wickets. But Lance Cairns got three, Stephen Boock four and Ewen Chatfield four. The boys were lining up to bowl. The other key was that we caught really well behind the wicket.

England just weren't interested in being there. Except for Derek Randall, who reached 25 second time around, no one made 20 in either innings. There was time for a little humour — and we did have cause to giggle a little. I mean for heaven's sake . . . how often had we over the years enjoyed dominating top-class opposition to the point where victory was a certainty (weather permitting) a long way out?

Allan Lamb and Ian Botham are great mates on and off the field. That's been well documented over the years. They were batting together, briefly, and Lamb was on strike. He copped a shocker from Hadlee which just missed glove, nose, helmet . . . everything really. For Lamb, it was a genuinely scary split-second in life. For the rest of us knowing 'Lega' as we did, it was a little funnier. Botham was beaming at his mate's disgust.

Lamb's reply was, as always, short and sharp. 'Jesus, Both, I tasted the bloody leather on that one.' That was indeed the final straw for the Poms because that particular touring party enjoyed supping their Cloudy Bay with a full complement of teeth and jaws unwired.

I thought the England attitude was summed up by what their captain, Willis,

Richard Hadlee . . . match-winning 99.

wrote later: 'Yes, we did bowl some of the biggest tripe I have ever seen in test cricket, and yes, we should have made over 100 in each innings. But to lose a test series on the flip of a coin on a 5000-piece jigsaw was particularly galling.'

That was the difference that week. The wicket was bad for both teams. We did the best we could in the circumstances; they seemed to regard it as beneath them to roll up their sleeves and fight it out. We made over 300; they had two tries and never got to 100. But, then again, we did have a player named Hadlee on our team.

66. All aboard the Love Boat

Great shipboard romances

I reckon some of these old cricketers got up to a lot more than they like to let on. Take the 1937 team to England, for instance. Eric Tindill got married on the day the team left, but had to leave behind his wife Mary. Though Mary had family in Ireland and was going to stay with them while the cricket tour took place, she was not permitted to sail on the same boat as the team.

So while Eric took a berth on the *Arawa*, Mary was forced to wait a week or two and take the next boat to Britain. Evidently that ensured that Eric's thoughts would be focused more firmly on cricket!

Imagine how he felt, then, on that voyage to England, when he watched two of his team-mates, Lindsay Weir and Walter Hadlee, develop strong shipboard romances. Two young Auckland women, Betty Blanchard and Lilla Monro, had decided to undertake what in those days was surely the adventure of a lifetime and were travelling on the *Arawa* too.

There must have been some strong chemistry about because marriage followed for both pairs, and what marriages. At the time of writing, both had passed their 60-year mark.

I did like the story Lilla tells. She says that she and Betty boarded the boat first, in Wellington, and were leaning over the handrail perusing the talent among the cricket team when the players boarded. They watched all 15 players and manager Tom Lowry board and then one woman turned to the other and said: 'And there's not a good-looking one among them!'

67. Jumping to cricketing conclusions

When the journos get it wrong, they really get it wrong!

Despite their best endeavours, journalists will make mistakes, as do the players they write about. There have been some funny and memorable blunders down the years, but two particularly humorous ones occurred during the 2001–2 season.

The Christchurch *Press* gained unwanted headlines when a punt it took on the outcome of a one-day international match in Australia went wrong. In a preliminary match of the tri-series, Australia were 82–6 chasing New Zealand's imposing 245–8 when the *Press* reached deadline time.

Across its back page, the 'Press' went big with its overline: 'Black Caps stretch winning streak to five straight over world champs'. An eye-catching main headline read: 'NZ sends Aussies crashing'.

Even as the first edition was being transported to North Canterbury and beyond, Michael Bevan was leading a brilliant Australian revival. At about midnight (New Zealand time), Bevan reached his century and, with support from Shane Warne and Brett Lee, guided Australia to an unlikely victory.

54 Wednesday, January 30, 2002

Black Caps stretch winning streak

NZ sends Aussies crashing

The Christchurch *Press* jumps the gun.

A few months later Joseph Romanos, my co-author, informed readers of his *Listener* Sportstalk column of a sensational new Namibian fast bowler named !Kabbo (the ! symbol apparently indicated a clicking sound difficult to reflect in English spelling).

Listener readers were told that !Kabbo stood just 1.52 metres tall and was a member of the San tribe of Kalahari Bushmen in southern Africa. His family was part of a group of San who were forced off their traditional homeland by settlers in the 1920s and had lived in a remote part of Namibia since.

Romanos wrote about how the San tribe's exposure to Europeans in the 1920s introduced them to cricket, how rudiments of the game had survived down the years and how three years ago a Canadian anthropologist, Loof Lirpa, discovered the San and was intrigued by their strange games.

It was a marvellous story, going on to describe the discovery of !Kabbo, a sensationally fast bowler who shuffled in off three paces and delivered thunderbolts at an estimated 160 km/h. At a special trial arranged by Namibian cricket officials, !Kabbo proved too fast for all the leading Namibian batsmen. Romanos suggested readers keep an eye out for !Kabbo at the 2003 World Cup in South Africa.

There was just one problem with the story, which Romanos found on the Cricinfo website. The name of the Canadian anthropologist should have alerted him, and so should the date the story was posted, 1 April.

It was a chastened Romanos who informed *Listener* readers a couple of weeks later that he'd been duped by an April Fool's joke. He promised he would be more sceptical in future.

68. Wads to the rescue — well, almost

Battling with the Bangalore belly

New Zealand cricket followers will recall the test against India at Bangalore in November 1988 for one reason: it was there that Richard Hadlee passed Ian Botham's record and became test cricket's highest wicket-taker.

It was certainly an emotion-charged day and when Richard got rid of Indian opener Arun Lal in his third over, caught by Chris Kuggeleijn in the gully, we were all delighted for him. That record had become such a focus in the lead-up to the test that it was a relief when it fell and we could get back to the business of playing test cricket. Richard, typically, didn't stop there, but finished the innings with 5–65.

But I don't recall that game in Bangalore just for Richard's special moment. It was also the match in which our team was decimated by illness, to the extent that we were casting about the commentary box and anywhere else for replacement players.

There was a rest day slotted in after the third day. It proved fatal for our test chances because during the day 12 members of our team were struck down with such a severe virus that we had to spend the day in bed. It was a virus that made us shiver, vomit and dry-retch and it brought on terrible diarrhoea.

Even coach Bob Cunis didn't escape. One of the most amusing memories for us all, and it was funny only after all were well again, was the sight of Bob emerging from his room at one stage limping worse than ever and eyes squinting to the point he was looking distinctly Chinese. He looked awful, or in his words, 'near death', but in typical hard-man Cunis fashion, barked, 'The bastards are not going to send me home in a box!'

Those who escaped painted white crosses on the sick players' hotel doors and walked around ringing a bell, wailing, 'Bring out your dead.' As I said, it's funny now.

Anyway, when play resumed on day four, we were already in a bit of trouble at 145–6, replying to their 384. Hadlee, not out overnight, could not take his place at the crease and Kuggeleijn was very unwell too. Both of them remained behind at the hotel, too ill even to get out of their beds.

I was one of the not-out batsmen and was joined by trusty Ewen Chatfield. We managed to put on 34 before I was lbw to Kapil Dev. As our partnership progressed, it became obvious that we had a chance of avoiding the follow-on, so John Wright, our captain, rang the hotel and asked Hadlee and Kuggeleijn to get down to the ground and do their best.

Kuggeleijn attempted to bat, but was out first ball and out wobbled Hadlee, really struggling. He was dizzy and not with it at all. In fact, amazingly for such a stats man, he didn't even know exactly how many were needed to avoid the follow-on. He took a two-eyed stance, to help him, he said, see the ball better. He slashed at one from Kapil and it flew behind square for four and got us past the follow-on, before he was bowled.

Then followed the amazing sight of Kapil supporting one of Richard's shoulders and helping him limp from the park. Richard was completely spent. It was truly a pathetic sight.

When India batted, we may have created a world record by using no fewer than five substitute fieldsmen at the same time. These included not only Tony Blain, Danny Morrison and Bert Vance, who were not in our playing XI, but also TVNZ news commentator Ken Nicholson and Jeremy Coney, who was covering the tour for Radio New Zealand.

Jeremy's credentials were well known, and he was only a year out of international cricket. Ken had played for Otago in the early 1970s and his real mission on tour was to capture the magic moment on film of the Hadlee world record.

He actually proved a handy man in the covers and did chase some serious leather for a short period of time. After India declared, he was buzzing — it had been a real thrill for him.

It wasn't such a thrill for the retired Coney, who said later: 'I stood in the slips and looked at the off-side field. None of us had been selected in the side.'

The matter of the replacement fieldsmen became quite comical. We were sure that Bryan Waddle, the Radio New Zealand commentator who'd been on tour so often with us, was dead keen to get out onto the field. Bryan had played senior club cricket in Wellington and we felt he fancied himself a bit as a cricketer. Certainly Wads has often over the years hinted at net sessions that he was more than capable and showed a lot of ticker when on strike in the bouncy WACA nets in Perth on a couple of occasions.

He'd regard it as a coup if he could say he'd taken the field for New Zealand in a test.

News Media Auckland

Bryan Waddle . . . still waiting.

So we made quite a show of expressing our panic at the dire position we were in and casting around looking for substitutes. Bryan was bursting to help, and seemed quite miffed when we asked Ken to field for us. In fact, miffed isn't the word. He was downright annoyed!

I think that's as close as Wads has come to playing for New Zealand, although he has appeared for press elevens around the world and rumour has it he was Man of the Match once in Trinidad.

Footnote: from time to time, various New Zealand team officials have filled in during minor tour games. Manager Murray Chapple even appeared in a first-class match when New Zealand toured the West Indies in 1972. In 1984, our team doctor, Richard Edmond (we nicknamed him Dr Doom because he was always giving us a list of Dos and Don'ts with dire warnings accompanying each), fielded for us during the test at Karachi, and received a terrific crack on the shins for his trouble.

69. When even managers were Young Guns

Age no barrier for Chats, Chapple and co.

Cricket team managers are supposed to be wise old heads. They've been through it all many times before and on tour are able to offer their wisdom and experience to the young players they're looking after.

But there was one occasion when a New Zealand touring team had a manager who was younger than one of the players. In the West Indies in 1972, Murray Chapple, born on 25 July 1930, was the manager. He was a fortnight younger than the team's leg-spinner, Jack Alabaster.

This has almost happened on the odd other occasion, as well. In 1961–2 Gordon Leggat managed the New Zealand team to South Africa. He was born only a year before one of the players, Zin Harris.

And in England in 1986, Ewen Chatfield became an excellent team manager when Bob Vance, the appointed manager, was taken ill and had to return home. Chats had hurt his thumb and was out of action anyway, so it worked out well. He just happened to be the oldest member of the touring team, a year older than Richard Hadlee.

We could have sent for a new manager, but the team decided unanimously that Chats would be ideal, and he was. I've often reflected on how under-utilised Chats has been by New Zealand Cricket. He would make a really good manager of the New Zealand team. He has excellent skills and disciplines, is an experienced player himself, would be a good shoulder to cry on and — very important — is lacking in puffery and ego.

70. It was quick, Rod, but not that quick

Quinny winds up the radar . . . and the commentators

There's no doubt that the advent of the speedball radar has enhanced television coverage of cricket. It adds another dimension to the viewers' understanding of the game, and is often a useful talking point for commentators. There's a particular fascination with watching the speed of the really fast bowlers, as they get above 140 km/h and even 150 km/h. Australian Brett Lee and Pakistani Shoaib Akhtar have even on occasion hovered around the 160 km/h mark.

However, from my observations, there is a disparity between the speedball radar readings in different countries, so perhaps it is wise to treat the speeds with just a degree of suspicion, as this story about portly Canterbury batsman Rod Latham illustrates.

It happened at Hamilton in January 1993, and it involved Keith Quinn. What a true lover and supporter of New Zealand sport is the Quinnster, as he is sometimes known these days. He has been a legendary commentator in many fields over the years for Television New Zealand, his versatility taking him from rugby to Olympics, tennis to athletics. For some years, Quinny would spend his 'off-season' in the production truck guiding TVNZ's international cricket coverage. Part of his job was to monitor the speedball radar readings and relay them to the graphics operator so they could be posted to the viewer at home.

So we get back to the test in Hamilton. New Zealand, needing 127 to win, was bowled out for 93, the swing and speed of Wasim Akram and Waqar Younis, who took five wickets each, being too good.

On the fourth evening, Quinny spent an enjoyable hour or two in the Trust Bank

News Media Auckland

Rod Latham . . . had to contend with a 'rocket' from Waqar Younis.

Park pavilion with Rod Latham, Mark Greatbatch and Chris Kuggeleijn, taking part in an impromptu sports quiz session. Afterwards he reflected on what good company the cricketers had been.

The next morning Wasim and Waqar ripped through New Zealand's batting, and the speedball radar consistently revealed speeds in the 137–139 range. Latham, batting at No 6, was bowled by one of Waqar's trademark inswinging rockets for a duck. The reading came through at 138 km/h — quick enough in anyone's language. But the graphic came up reading 146 km/h — lightning pace.

Producer: 'What's with the difference, Quinny?'

Quinn: 'C'mon mate, Roddy's a great bloke, and he plays rugby.'

Keith thought he would do his bit to repay Latham for the pleasant company the previous evening, so bumped up the speedball radar recording for the fatal delivery. The Television New Zealand commentators noted the 146 and became most animated. There were comments such as, 'No wonder Latham missed that one. It was an absolute rocket. He was desperately unlucky to have to face a missile like that so early in his innings.'

It didn't make any difference to the score, but at least it meant critics went a little easier on Latham.

71. Ad-Vancing the run rate

Wellington tactics frowned upon — from as far away as Lord's!

The actions of Wellington captain Erv McSweeney and senior player Bert Vance during their team's 1990 Shell Trophy clash with Canterbury at Lancaster Park caused all sorts of debate. Some people felt McSweeney and Vance had made a farce of the match and brought cricket into disrepute. Others praised them for their innovation and daring.

MCC officials at Lord's became involved, refusing to consider statistics from the match for records purposes, and controversy raged for weeks. Heaven knows what the reaction would have been if Radio Sport, with its talkback segment, had existed then.

What happened? Wellington, seeking a win to capture the Shell Trophy, trailed on the first innings, but fought back well and eventually set Canterbury a target of 291 to win in 59 overs. The home team slumped to 108–8 with 30 overs remaining, and Wellington's prospects looked bright.

However, Lee Germon and Roger Ford then built a long partnership that looked like seeing Canterbury through to a draw. They batted out the next 28 overs without too many problems. So, with two overs remaining, Canterbury were 196–8.

In an effort to belatedly get Canterbury back into the game and then perhaps entice the batsmen into error, McSweeney had Vance bowl an over that eventually conceded 77 runs. Without any run-up, Vance bowled overarm lobbed full tosses and deliberate no-balls. The over contained 22 deliveries, of which only five (second, 18th, 19th, 21st and 22nd) were legitimate balls. Evan Gray bowled the last over and this contained five deliberate no-balls and cost 17 runs.

Amid all the confusion, neither the official scorers nor the scoreboard attendants were able to keep pace. There was utter chaos. Therefore Ford was unaware that when he faced the final ball of the match, the scores were level and, as it transpired, one run would have given Canterbury not only victory in the match, but also the Shell Trophy. Ford padded away the final delivery.

There were all sorts of goings-on, arguments and discussions at Lancaster Park that evening and the official figures didn't become available until 8.40 pm.

Vance's over (with Germon facing) read: 0, 4, 4, 4, 6, 6, 4, 6, 1, 4, 1, 0, 6, 6, 6, 6, 6, 0, 0, 4, 0, 1. Germon was caught from the first and 12th deliveries, which were no-balls. During this over, Germon moved from 75 to 145 and Canterbury's ninth-wicket record was smashed, but no one was sure what the precise total was.

Gray's final over (again with Germon facing), read: 4, 4, 2, 1, 1, 0, 0, 2, 0, 1, 0. Germon was bowled by the ninth ball, a no-ball.

Cricket is a game in which statistics play an integral part, but, of course, what went on at Lancaster Park that day made a mockery of statistics. Germon was credited with 160 not out, scored in 152 minutes from 143 balls, with eight sixes and 16 fours. Never has a first-class century been gifted to a player in such extraordinary circumstances.

Ironically, Wellington ended up winning the Shell Trophy anyway. They had four points deducted for a slow over rate after the Christchurch circus, but beat Central Districts outright in the final round to win the title.

I'd be lying if I said I'd never been involved in matches where runs had been gifted to keep batting teams interested in a run chase.

Captains often introduce part-time bowlers to try to buy wickets, knowing it might cost a few quick runs but hoping an established batsman may momentarily relax and become reckless.

What happened that day in Christchurch stretched all those sorts of theories way beyond the limit. The MCC were right to regard it the way they did. No doubt if it had been televised it would have been bizarre viewing. If the scorers had so much trouble keeping up, even legendary radio commentator Peter Sharp's talents would have been sorely tested!

Knowing Lee Germon, I wouldn't imagine he'd be over-the-moon proud of his 160. Of great interest, though, would be how Ervin McSweeney would handle it today, now

News Media Auckland

Bert Vance . . . history's most unsuccessful bowler.

that he's the highly respected boss of Wellington Cricket. Evan Gray was a little hard to read at the best of times. Bert Vance was involved in the odd controversial incident, but I always felt he might have regretted the Christchurch business and I later discovered when researching this book that this was the case.

'It wasn't really my way of doing things,' said Bert. 'I wasn't a cricketer who ever liked to gift a run, no matter what the circumstance. I liked to play it hard. We thought we were going to bowl out Canterbury that day. The wicket was flat, but we had them eight down, then Lee Germon and Roger Ford had a long partnership. Lee batted really well. Erv decided we would give away the runs.

'At first Tim Ritchie was going to bowl the over, but I didn't think that was a good idea, even though Tim himself was keen. I said to Erv, "You can't let a young guy do this. There's going to be all sorts of trouble. It's better if I do it." So I bowled the over. I can't say I enjoyed it. I took a run-up for the first few deliveries, then just stood there and bowled no-balls.

'I felt sorry for Lee. He'd batted exceptionally well, but now the innings is remembered for the runs he was gifted.'

Bert says he did, indeed, get plenty of feedback afterwards. 'It's quite funny looking back, but there was a lot of feeling at the time. I got two letters from the MCC. One bloke, Colonel somebody with a hyphen in his name, said he knew my father and what a fine, upstanding person he was. He said my father would have been ashamed to have raised a scoundrel like me!'

72. Sparkling display on the Emerald Isle

No luck for the Irish back in '37

The New Zealand team that toured Britain in 1937 didn't have an especially happy time of it, losing the test series and struggling even to win games against the counties. However, they did set one record that has stood unchallenged since.

Never has a New Zealand team won a first-class match as quickly as did Curly Page's side in their end-of-tour fixture against Ireland. It must be said that the Irish lineup was of dubious quality — a look through the names does not reveal any test players, or even any who made a name for themselves at first-class level.

Still, the game, played in Dublin, was accorded first-class status and allotted three days. Ireland batted first on a dodgy wicket and made 79, Alby Roberts, Norm Gallichan, Bill Carson and Sonny Moloney all boosting their tour averages with some cheap wickets. Ireland's 79 didn't look too bad when the New Zealand team crumbled to be dismissed for 64. Jimmy Boucher, the Ireland captain, took 7–13 and the whole innings occupied just 32 overs.

So, as quickly as that, Ireland were back batting again. This time Jack Cowie, the New Zealand team's one world-class bowler that season, really got stuck in. From eight overs he took 6–3 and Ireland were all out for 30. There were seven ducks and the innings lasted just 18 overs.

New Zealand returned to the crease and Tom Lowry, who was officially designated manager of this team, ended the farce by smashing 30 not out as New Zealand roared to 46–2 to win the game by eight wickets.

This is one of the very rare occasions when a first-class match has been completed in one day. I can find only one other instance of it occurring since 1925.

73. Craftsman, captain, coach, commentator

Glenn Turner — an enigmatic cricketing career

New Zealand cricket has produced some diverse and interesting characters down the years, but surely no one so split loyalties and caused more controversy than Glenn Maitland Turner. I played with and against Glenn in my early years in first-class and international cricket, was the wicketkeeper when he had his first stint as the New Zealand coach, and later worked alongside him in the commentary box.

In every area of cricket, he has divided opinion.

If we look at him first as a player, some will say he was the finest batsman produced by New Zealand. He scored 103 first-class centuries, had that fantastic 1972 tour of the West Indies when he scored four double-centuries, two of them in tests, made 1000 runs before the end of May in 1973, scored centuries in each innings of the test in Christchurch in 1974 when we beat Australia for the first time, became one of the world's great one-day batsmen . . . it's an impressive list.

By New Zealand standards this record should put him in the hero category — but has he ever been regarded in that way? New Zealand's cricket game started to come of age in the late 1970s and early 1980s. New heroes were found — Turner's non-appearance meant he was largely forgotten.

He withdrew from test cricket in 1977, when he was 29 years of age, and basically didn't play the game again at that level (with the exception of a couple of tests against Sri Lanka in 1983, right at the end of his career). What on earth was New Zealand's best batsman doing working season after season in the commentary box when the test team needed him?

His detractors will tell you that he was never good against fast bowling, that all his famous innings came against attacks in which the opposition had no real speedster.

Certainly by withdrawing from test cricket, Turner missed out on series where he would have got to sample the delights of a young Imran Khan, Roberts, Holding, Garner and Croft of the West Indies, Thomson and Lillee and so on. He did not bat very well against Lillee in 1977, the last series he played before placing himself in test exile.

When he made his runs in the West Indies, the pace attack was led by Vanburn Holder, Uton Dowe and an ageing Garfield Sobers. That predated the days of Roberts, Holding, Malcolm Marshall and the rest of them. So maybe there's something to be said for the 'didn't like fast bowling' theory. You can go too far down this line, though. It's hard to imagine he played 15 years of county cricket and 41 test matches and didn't encounter his share of quick bowlers on green tracks.

> **I've never met any batsman, no matter how good, who really relished genuinely fast bowling, of the Akhtar-Lee-Marshall pace. Famous England opening batsman Herbert Sutcliffe once said: 'Nobody likes it; some just hide the fact better.' Maybe Glenn didn't hide the fact as well.**

I've no doubt he had the technical ability and the determination to play pace bowling as well as anyone. In terms of New Zealand batsmen I've seen — so this is from about 1970 on — I put Martin Crowe at the top. To me, he is out by himself, the way he could play spin and pace, one-day cricket and tests, on all sorts of wickets. But Glenn is not far away. He had a very tight technique, good judgement of what to play and what not to play, a wide enough range of scoring strokes, the ability to concentrate for long spells and, as he showed in some of his great one-day innings, flair and the ability to improvise.

It's just terribly sad that he chose not to play tests for New Zealand for so long. To me, that puts an asterisk against him as a player. Once batsmen get to the level of a Crowe or a Turner, they are judged by their international results and Glenn removed himself. Young batsmen like Bruce Edgar, John Wright, John F Reid, Martin and Jeff Crowe could have done with his experience and advice in their early years of test cricket, but he wasn't in the dressing room.

So that's Turner the batsman. Make your own judgement. I've seen him tear apart opposing attacks — remember that one-day series against England in New Zealand in 1983 when he smashed 88, 94 and 34 — and when I was at college I listened to Tony Cozier's magnificent commentaries of his epic test innings in the West Indies. But I can't reconcile someone of his ability pulling out of test cricket at the age of 29. He was a great player who didn't play.

As a coach, he was also a mixture. Perhaps he was lucky with his timing in his first spell as coach, from 1985–87. He took charge of a team that had in Richard Hadlee a genuine match-winner. There was a core of players who by then had plenty of experience at test level and had the confidence to tackle any team in the world, players like Jeremy Coney, Bruce Edgar, John Wright, Ewen Chatfield and John Bracewell. And he had in Martin Crowe a batsman who could score centuries against the world's best. The batting could be built around Martin.

That's not to take anything away from Glenn, though. He definitely helped us in those years. He assisted players technically — even the great Hadlee spoke of how Glenn had helped him by advising him to bowl from closer to the stumps. And he didn't hand out praise lightly. So when you got some praise from Glenn, you knew he meant it.

Sometimes I felt he was inclined to be too negative. He would say he was merely being realistic, but it was a weakness in his personality that he did not seek to praise more. Cricketers, like any sportsmen, need confidence, and sometimes they need a bit of a boost. You can take this too far with over-the-top praise for not very much, but Glenn erred the other way.

Strangely, though, it was a day that Glenn really got behind us and supported us that resulted in one of New Zealand's best efforts ever in test cricket. We were in Brisbane before the first test of the 1985 series and Glenn delivered a very unGlenn-like team talk. In our team meeting at the Park Royal Hotel, he told us in no uncertain terms that man for man we were better than the Aussies. He spoke about all our strengths — our long batting lineup, our ability to take wickets, our team spirit, our ability to close up a game and play tight, our sharp fielding. It was all pretty mind-boggling at the time, coming from Glenn, and it certainly gave us a huge lift.

If Glenn really thought we could beat the Aussies — and he wouldn't have said it if he didn't — then, bring them on! Well, we went out and played almost the perfect test and put them away by an innings. Richard Hadlee took his nine wickets in an innings, 15 in the match. There were centuries from Martin Crowe and John Reid and everyone chipped in. It was a total team performance and we really thrashed them. The players did it, but Glenn must get plenty of credit, too.

One funny incident I recall from the 1985 tour of Australia occurred during the second test in Sydney. Some of our batsmen had been having trouble playing leg-spin — Bob Holland had taken 8–33 for New South Wales in the first innings against us

Glenn Turner the batsman . . . masterful.

the previous week. Glenn decided the sweep shot was at the root of the problem, so he banned the sweep. It was not to be played at all, under any circumstances. That team meeting in Sydney was of a far less positive nature.

John Bracewell was called into the team late. He arrived just in time for the test in Sydney and, not having been present when the no-sweeping edit was issued, proceeded to sweep with impunity, and no little success. Batting at No 10, Braces swept his way to 83 not out, putting on 124 runs for the 10th wicket with Stephen Boock. Holland, who had taken six cheap wickets, was smashed all around the Sydney Cricket Ground.

Braces and Turner always had an interesting relationship. I remember a practice at the Oval one day in 1983, prior to the World Cup match against England, when Braces beamed Glenn on purpose. Braces was never one to respect reputations and it would have counted for nothing to him that Glenn had been in the New Zealand team since 1969.

Turner had repeatedly hit Bracewell into the roof of the net at an angle that meant the ball would rebound down threatening the bowler. After a while Bracewell had had enough and obliged with a sharpish beamer. Turner ducked, retrieved the ball from the net behind and proceeded to send the bowler from the nets back to the dressing room, advising him that he thought he had not reached the peak of his maturity.

From 1985–7, Glenn coached New Zealand teams that won series at home and away against Australia, beat England in England and drew with world champions the West Indies. You can't argue with that record. He didn't get on with every player — for instance, Lance Cairns and Glenn never really saw eye to eye. But he had a tremendous relationship with Coney, his captain, and they formed a mighty effective team.

However, it was all very different when he had another spell as coach, in 1995–6. This time he wasn't taking over a team of experienced players and there was no Hadlee to make life miserable for opposing batsmen. It was a very young team, and, from my observation, an immature one. Some of the players in that group — Cairns, Parore, Fleming, Astle, Nash — went on to be fine test players, but at the time they were only just starting out.

They needed some very careful man-management. It must be said that some of them seemed amazingly juvenile. Worse, Turner was taking over after a particularly low moment for New Zealand cricket. There'd been the disastrous tour of South Africa, with all the discipline problems, and then the repeated losses at home during New Zealand's centenary summer.

Under coach Geoff Howarth, there had been very little discipline in the team and it showed in the results. Turner was brought in to fix that, but maybe he went too far. He was 10 years older than last time he was coach and was therefore more removed from the players. They were in their early 20s; he was approaching 50.

He decided he didn't want Ken Rutherford as his captain, so he dropped him. This was quite a decision. Ken had been Player of the Year the previous season, yet lost not only the captaincy but also his test spot. Martin Crowe and Danny Morrison were two other senior players. Both were having their own problems with injury, and I'm not sure how well Glenn related to them.

The Crowe-Turner relationship seemed uneasy. There was a problem over a fitness test Martin apparently failed on Eden Park No 2 before the 1995 World Cup and I know Martin didn't appreciate some of Glenn's discipline measures, such as filling out individual performance reports and having 'naughty boy' nets.

It was at this time Glenn was assembling a selection panel. Even though we had our differences, he asked me to put my name forward as a candidate, which, after due consideration, I did. His theory was that I was touring overseas a lot with the New Zealand team in a television commentary role, and therefore seeing the team perform a lot in different conditions. He also considered we shared the same thought patterns in a few areas.

Glenn Turner the coach . . . mixed reviews.

It eventually came to nothing as the powers that be deemed it inappropriate to pick a team then earn money commentating about its performance. Those theories have obviously changed of late. Lesley Murdoch is convenor of the New Zealand women's team selection panel and is often used as a radio and television commentator. Peter Sharp, long-time radio man and former Television New Zealand commentator, is on the board of New Zealand Cricket and has kept his job at the mike.

Glenn removed Adam Parore from the wicketkeeping role, telling him that he would need to hold his place as a specialist batsman, and installed Lee Germon as captain and wicketkeeper-batsman. This caused resentment as most players felt Germon was a Turner puppet, that he was not a test player on merit.

I could see what Glenn was doing. He wanted to instil some authority and discipline and had to have a captain he could work with. But the players didn't really buy into the idea. Some childish stuff went on as both captain and coach were undermined.

The situation became intolerable and on the 1996 tour of the West Indies, Cairns and Parore both walked out, citing injury. Turner had problems with other players too, including Dion Nash and Roger Twose. Justin Vaughan was called in as a replacement and given a vice-captaincy role ahead of many more senior players. It was a crisis and New Zealand Cricket reacted by dispensing with Turner's services, replacing him with Steve Rixon.

In hindsight, it was a successful move. Players like Cairns and Parore, on the verge of being lost to the New Zealand team, went on to become world-class players, and the team's results gradually picked up. But Turner was very resentful. He said some derogatory things about New Zealand Cricket Chief Executive Christopher Doig and then put out a book, *Lifting The Covers*, which examined the whole unsavoury business from his perspective.

The Turner affair has rumbled on and in 2002 both Parore and Cairns released biographies in which they revisited those tempestuous times and were extremely critical of Turner.

I wouldn't place all the blame at Glenn's feet. The players should look at their actions and ask themselves honestly if their actions were mature and in the best interests of representing New Zealand with honour. After all, it must be a pretty drastic step to leave your team-mates mid-tour. But Turner must take some of the responsibility for what happened. It's one thing to be big on discipline and to try to bring order, but there must always be room for flexibility, for treating players differently. They are not Glenn's strengths.

Glenn stayed involved with cricket through his television commentating and, after his controversial exit from the coaching job, his work behind the microphone, which was always excellent, was scrutinised closely. How would he treat Rixon, Parore,

Cairns and the rest? Glenn would say he called it as he saw it, that he was impartial. I felt there was an edge there. That would be only human, after what had gone on.

He was never one to offer praise lightly when commentating, but after 1996 the praise, never a torrent in the first place, turned into no more than a trickle. I often sensed he was more prepared to say that the opposition had played poorly than that New Zealand had played well. After being sacked, human nature would presume at times he simply didn't want New Zealand to do well. I might be completely wrong in assuming this, but I don't think so.

When Television New Zealand lost the rights to broadcast domestic cricket to the Sky Network, Turner was dropped as a commentator. He continued to do some commentary work overseas, and is now used extensively as a radio commentator. Sky built its own team of commentators and Turner was not among them.

Glenn has gone on to coach Otago. It's good that someone of his experience has remained involved in New Zealand cricket, but was it significant that after he became coach, Otago lost several of its New Zealand representatives to other provinces, including Paul Wiseman, Matthew Horne and Mark Richardson?

In a way, the Glenn Turner story is a slightly sad one. As a teenager, he would get up in the middle of the night to do a bread run to earn money to get to England so he could pursue a career as a professional player. He made himself into a great batsman. He accrued a vast amount of knowledge during his time in England.

And yet he got himself involved in bitter wrangles with all sorts of people. He and Walter Hadlee, the chairman of the New Zealand Cricket Council board, were poles apart and at one stage Turner was even suspended after a row over airfares. He advocated strongly for the players to be paid better and was the first of the modern breed of New Zealand professional cricketers, treading a path soon to be followed by Geoff Howarth, John Parker, David O'Sullivan, Richard Hadlee, John Wright, Martin Crowe and others.

He has been one of the most pivotal and influential figures in New Zealand cricket for more than three decades. He is always intelligent company, an interesting person to have a dinner with. But he has always marched to the beat of his own drum, and in the end this has cost him, in terms of popularity and jobs.

Like it or lump it, on or off the field New Zealand cricket has never got the best out of Glenn Maitland Turner. Quite frankly, in a well of talent so shallow at times, it has been a bloody waste!

About the authors

IAN SMITH played 63 test matches and 98 one-day internationals for New Zealand, from 1980–92. At the time of his retirement he held the New Zealand record for most dismissals in test matches by a wicketkeeper. He made 426 dismissals in first-class cricket, which is still the record for a New Zealand wicketkeeper. Besides his wicketkeeping ability, Smith scored two test centuries, including a never-to-be-forgotten 173 against India at Eden Park, and captained New Zealand in one test. Since retiring, he has been a television commentator, covering primarily cricket and rugby. He has commentated cricket for Television New Zealand and the Sky Network in New Zealand, for Channel 9 in Australia, for Channel Four in Britain and for TWI in India and the West Indies.

JOSEPH ROMANOS is one of New Zealand's leading sports writers. He has written a weekly sports column for the *Listener* magazine since 1989 and is a regular contributor to other publications, as well as working for Radio Sport, Radio New Zealand and Television New Zealand. This is the 30th book he has written or helped write. Among that number are seven on cricket, including biographies of Walter Hadlee, Martin Crowe, John Reid and Merv Wallace.